Authors
of Pictures,
Draughtsmen
of Words

Authors of Pictures, Draughtsmen of Words

Ruth Hubbard

Lewis & Clark College

Heinemann
Portsmouth, NH

Heinemann Educational Books, Inc.
70 Court Street   Portsmouth, NH 03801
Offices and agents throughout the world

The following have generously given permission to use quotations from published works:

Pages 10–11: Excerpt from *The Little Prince* by Antoine de Saint-Exupéry, copyright 1943 and renewed 1971 by Harcourt Brace Jovanovich, Inc., reprinted by permission of the publisher.

Pages 11–12 and Figure 1–1: Reprinted with permission from R. Burns and S. H. Kaufman, *Actions, Styles, and Symbols in Kinetic Family Drawings (K-F-D): An Interpretive Manual* (New York: Brunner/Mazel, 1972), p. 174 and Figure K-F-D-77.

Figures 3–1 and 3–2: From W. Hudson, "Pictorial Depth Perception in Subcultural Groups in Africa," *Journal of Social Psychology* 52 (1960). Figures P1, P2, P10, and P11 (pp. 186–87). Reprinted with permission of the Helen Dwight Reid Educational Foundation. Published by Heldref Publications, 4000 Albemarle St., N. W., Washington, D.C. 20016. Copyright © 1960.

Figure 3–5: From Ellen Winner, *Invented Worlds: The Psychology of the Arts* (Cambridge: Harvard University Press, 1982), p. 89. Reprinted by permission of Harvard University Press.

Figure 3–11: "Madonna Surrounded by Saints," the Aldobrini Triptych. Collection of the Portland Art Museum, Oregon; gift of the Samuel H. Kress Foundation.

Figure 4–1: From H. F. Duncan, N. Gourlay, and W. Hudson, *A Study of Pictorial Perception Among Bantu and White Primary School Children in South Africa* (Johannesburg: Witwatersrand University Press, 1973), p. 26. Human Sciences Research Council Series no. 31. Reprinted by permission of Witwatersrand University Press.

Figure 4–9: "Satyr Pursuing a Maenad" (Attic Red Figure). Collection of the Portland Art Museum, Oregon; The Sally Lewis Collection of Classical Antiquities.

Figure 4–15: Smilby, cartoon from *Punch*, February 1, 1956, p. 177. Reproduced by permission of *Punch*.

Every effort has been made to contact the copyright holders and the children and their parents for permission to reprint borrowed material. We regret any oversights that may have occurred and would be happy to rectify them in future printings of this work.

Library of Congress Cataloging-in-Publication Data

Hubbard, Ruth, 1950–
    Authors of pictures, draughtsmen of words / Ruth Hubbard.
        p. cm.
    Bibliography: p.
    ISBN 0–435–08491–7
    1. Visual literacy. 2. Learning, Psychology of. 3. Language
experience approach in education. 4. Reading (Elementary)—Language
experience approach. I. Title.
LB1068.H83   1989   88–34641
372.6—dc19   CIP

Designed by Maria Szmauz.

Cover photos by James Whitney.

Printed in the United States of America.

10 9 8 7 6 5 4 3 2 1

For Jim

who pulls together all my scattered fragments
and gives a home
to all the parts of me that were homeless.

contents

acknowledgments

As a way of publicly saying "thanks," I would like to acknowledge the many people who helped me in the research and writing of this book. My first thanks go, of course, to the children who gracefully tolerated my intrusions and allowed me to learn from them. I miss them already.

I am especially grateful to Pat McLure—teacher, advisor, colleague, and trusted friend. She welcomed me into her classroom and taught me to see what children *really* know. Her warmth, wisdom, and gentle humor have guided me for the past five years and will continue, I know, to enrich my life. Besides Pat, I was fortunate to have another close friend and colleague "in the field" with me—Brenda Miller. Because of our daily discussions, shared readings, and constant collaboration, Brenda's insights and ideas are throughout this work. She energized me with her hypotheses, cheered me up with her outrageous sense of humor, made me chicken soup when I was sick, soothed me with her poetry, and on top of that, she kept tossing good books my way, from Annie Dillard to Jeremy Rifkin. Thanks, Brenda!

I am also grateful to my Dissertation Committee, especially Jane Hansen and Donald Graves, for their encouragement and support. Rather than prescribing a traditional format for my work, they urged me to investigate what I was interested in and explore what I was learning through my writing. When we would meet to discuss the work in progress, the conversations I had with our diverse group—Jane Hansen, Donald Graves, Tom Newkirk, Deborah Stone, Doug Fricke, Pat McLure, and Brenda Miller—stimulated and nudged me forward.

I learned important writing and research lessons from Donald Murray, who encouraged me when I first began to look at visual and verbal literacy links. He taught me to follow what intrigues and surprises me, helping foster my love for research.

I also want to thank the many colleagues who read and thoughtfully responded to drafts of this manuscript. Linda Rief not only read excerpts, but generously met with me to discuss ideas and push my thinking forward. Donna Lee and Chip Nelson kindly allowed me to learn from them and their classroom after I had supposedly "withdrawn from the field." I am also grateful to Virginia Stuart, Peggy Murray, Elizabeth Chiseri-Strater, Judy Fueyo, and Gini Littlefield for their enthusiasm and their critical judgment.

The inspiration of Nancie Atwell's writing, teaching, and respect for young writers is also woven throughout the book. Her article "Writing and Reading from the Inside Out" opened my eyes to a new approach to literacy education, and with each new publication, my respect for her work grows. Even though she's younger than I am, I wish I could be Nancie Atwell when I grow up.

Warm thanks to Win Rhoades and Tom Romano for providing the perfect jazz tapes to write by—they got me through many a rough transition.

And finally, how can I thank my family for their endurance of a difficult year? It may take Meghan, Nathan, and Cory months to believe they can now play their music at the volume they'd prefer!

And Jim Whitney, my best friend and husband, helped me in every possible role—reading all my drafts, clarifying my thinking in late-night conversations, providing just the right metaphor, helping me with graphics, and poking fun at educational jargon when it reared its ugly head. Through everything, he continues to provide the solace and support only he can give me.

Words and Pictures— "They Both Have Their Own Uvantages"

Nick looks up from his writing and reads it out loud to the other three six-year-old boys who are working at the table with him: "When I play dinosaucers, the lowercase *m* is our enemy." He puts down the paper and explains, "I learned to make lowercase *m*. I like to make it, but it isn't really the dinosaucers' enemy. The pictures don't usually have letters, unless you have word bubbles" (Figure I−1).

Figure I−1   Nick's Writing: "When I play dinosaucers, the lowercase *m* is our enemy"

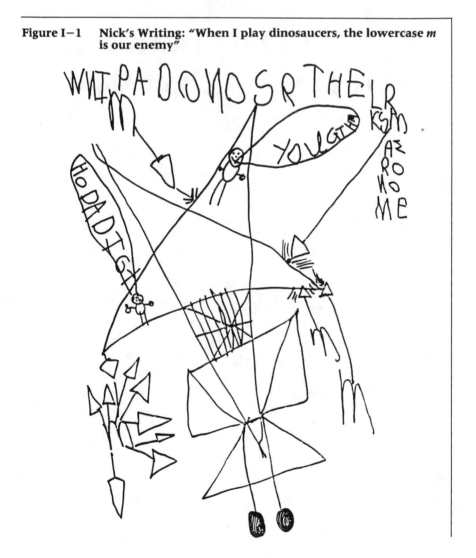

Eugene takes a break in coloring his harvest moon to comment, "If you do the picture first, then you have something in your mind that you could write. If you do the words first, then I don't know what to draw. But I think words can tell the story better."

"I don't think you can really read pictures," Paul comments. "Sometimes pictures can make it move, though, and the words don't do that."

"Words can tell a story a little better" is Ethan's comment. "But they both have their own uvantages. Pictures are sorta . . . they go together."

Eugene reconsiders. "I guess there's things pictures can do that . . . they really *can* tell the story, ya know. Sometimes, see, the pictures, like this one," he points to his moon, and reads, "'The day is over.' See, it looks like what the words do, but at a different angle."

In order to understand what they see and hear, young children have to attach meaning to the different patterns of light, shape, and color that they see, as well as organize the sounds into a linguistic system. By the time they come to school, children are able to create, and then share, this meaning through the use of various kinds of symbol systems. As they acquire literacy, they are hard at work, experimenting with, creating, and discussing the symbols they use to help formulate and communicate their ideas. And this is a difficult task, for "the blank sheet and salient edges of the page provide an immense number of potential 'degrees of freedom' which have to be reduced to workable order" (Freeman, 1977, p. 4).

As each of us attempts our search for meaning, we need a medium through which our ideas can take shape. But there is not just one medium; productive thought uses many ways to find meaning. Our ideas may take form in images, movement, or inner speech. Furthermore, the search for meaning begins young; crucial foundations for thinking patterns begin in childhood. In her pioneer work on creative thinking, Vera John-Steiner (1985) discusses the "inner languages" and symbol systems that adults employ as they think, but little investigation has been done of the symbolic strategies that young children use. This is unfortunate, since these strategies have enormous influence on emerging literacy skills.

In this book, I explore the symbol systems children create in the process of writing and reading. More specifically, I narrow my focus to two important systems: (1) pictorial, or visual, and (2) linguistic, or verbal. How do they work together? What influences help shape these symbol systems?

Symbols in Literacy: Too Much "Spinning Words about Words"

Educators, linguists, and cognitive psychologists alike have been stressing the importance of symbols and symbol theory in literacy for years. But the stress is almost always on the verbal symbol systems. As writer/artist Leo Lionni (1984) complains, "The study of literacy is all too often a matter of spinning words about words, without looking back to the images that precede words and to the feelings that precede both" (p. 732).

It isn't surprising that the field of literacy spends so much time "spinning words about words" since the supremacy of verbal thinking is the dominant view in this field. Hannah Arendt (1976) is not alone when she conjectures that "no speechless thought exists" (p. 100). Language is assumed in the literature to be the best vehicle for thought—perhaps even indispensable. Early in this century, for example, Wilhelm Herder (quoted in Arnheim, 1969) asserted that reflection is "only made possible by speech," and later Edward Sapir (1921), in his book on language, said that "thought may be a natural domain apart from the artificial one of speech, but speech would seem to be the only one we know of that leads to it" (p. 18). Benjamin Whorf (1956), too, stresses the primary role of language in thinking: "The world is presented in a kaleidoscope of impressions which has to be organized in our minds—and that means largely by a linguistic system" (p. 25).

Whorf touches on an important concept—the need for an organizational system to sort out the influx of stimuli we are exposed to. In essence, what we need is an inner symbol system to store and organize our thoughts. Most psychologists and educators stress the use of language in organizing thought (see Vygotsky, 1978; and Bruner, 1983). Jerome Bruner's work, in fact, depends only on models of thought that stress verbal stages. But does that inner system *need* to be linguistically based? There are voices of dissent.

Rudolf Arnheim (1969) stresses the importance of looking at visual as well as verbal thought. He contends, in fact, that the image is supreme: "Truly productive thinking in whatever area of cognition takes place in the realm of imagery" (p. v). Like Whorf, Vygotsky, and Bruner, Arnheim believes that in order to cope with the world, the mind must gather information and process it, but he stresses that in order to think about objects and events they must be available in the mind in some way. He believes that verbal thought—words alone—is secondary in shaping thought.

Visual thinking is considered by some psychologists to be as wired-in or preprogrammed as language. When infants explore their visual field, they scan the entire environment both to gain a perceptual context and to focus on specific details. They need to go back and forth between figure and foreground in order to "see." Their whirling, confused vision needs to be organized. Psychologist Ralph Haber (1966) points out that "to achieve knowledge of what they see, children have to attach meaning to the different patterns of light they perceive" (p. 338). This raw material of vision needs to be built into a mental framework. British psychologist Richard Gregory (1970) also defines perception in these terms: "Perception must, it seems, be a matter of seeing the present with stored objects of the past" (p. 10). And in a comprehensive review of symbolic representation theory, Gier Kauffmann (1985) concludes that "the ability to construct and act upon mental representations is regarded as the most fundamental property of human cognition" (p. 51).

But the division between visual and verbal oversimplifies the problem of how we shape and organize our thoughts. Most current theories fail to investigate the influences that help shape symbol systems, how these different systems change depending on the task at hand, or how they work together to *complement* each other.

Practitioners, on the other hand, often *do* stress the way words and pictures are intimately related. I took my title, for example, from e. e. cummings, who called himself "an author of pictures, a draughtsman of words." Besides practicing the craft of writing, cummings sketched and painted daily: oil

portraits of his wife and himself, watercolors of his farmhouse,
line drawings of elephants, anatomical studies of animals and
people. An interviewer once asked him, "Tell me, doesn't
your painting interfere with your writing?" He replied, "Quite
the contrary: they love each other dearly" (Hjerter, 1986,
p. 109). It was parallels like this that I could draw to my own
work as well as to that of young children that first intrigued
me, enticing me to begin to investigate the importance of
picture as well as word symbols in literacy.

Literacy Takes on New Meanings

Looking back in my journal, I can trace the genesis of this
study. I was struggling with the relationship between words
and images in my own work—trying to create a documentary
videotape. I had just read an interview with French filmmaker
Jean Rouch and was inspired by it:

> Rouch explains some of the problems he wrestles with in composing
> his films. I was especially interested in his discussion of the visual
> image and the narrative line—that they must work together and
> each have a special role in imparting the message. More than the
> struggles I'm having with [the videotape script], I thought of the
> kids in Pat's class—learning to read and write through creating
> picture books and reading those of adult authors. Just like I am,
> these children are discovering the relationship between verbal and
> visual language. What *is* the relationship between these words and
> images?. . . What are the limitations and opportunities of these
> relationships? Is anybody out there in Cognition Land looking at this
> stuff?   (February 28, 1985)

With the encouragement of Professor Donald Murray and
the members of my writing community, I began to explore
the relationship between words and images in my own video
work, in the writing of adult authors and illustrators, in
interviews with college students, *and,* most importantly, in
the emerging literacy of the six-year-old children in whose
classroom I was working. Sprinkled through my journal, I
find quotes that continue to fascinate me:

> I am finding that within my own mind there is a storehouse of
> images that can slowly be pulled out. . . .I can't insist on establishing
> a design or structure before writing because the inner images seem

harder to see than those of objects outside. Writing is like pulling for
minutes or hours on end on a fishing line. Something is coming up,
but I don't always know what it will be. In this case, perhaps it's best
to try freewriting as when the drawing hand guides itself across the
page.   (J. T., college freshman composition student)

First I put the whole picture in my head—a whole lot of pictures.
Then, I put them on paper, one by one. I already have the words
planned. I already know what I'm going to write about in the
morning. I make myself remember it all the time. I say it in my head
so people won't hear it. . . . I believe there's a wall in my head, like
this [she demonstrates]—there's halves—and there's words on one
side and pictures on the other.   (N. D., six-year-old student)

The pictures for me are a passionate affair with the words. . . . [In
picture books] you must never illustrate exactly what is written. You
must find a space in the text so that pictures can do the work. Then
you must let the words take over where words do it best. I like to
think of myself as setting words to pictures, for a true picture book is
a visual poem.   (Maurice Sendak, writer/illustrator)

   I was immersed in, fascinated with, and, unfortunately,
overwhelmed by the information I was collecting. A pilot
study that grew out of this exploration pointed the way to a
more organized and disciplined research study. The chapters
that follow describe the research I conducted that explored
more systematically the visual and verbal symbol systems that
children create in the process of writing and reading.
   This book has both a theoretical and methodological bias.
My view of artistic activity as basically a cognitive activity
is shaped largely by Ellen Winner (1982), Rudolf Arnheim
(1974), Nelson Goodman (1968), and Suzanne Langer (1942).
As Winner writes, "Both producing and perceiving art require
the ability to process and manipulate symbols and to make
extremely subtle discriminations. . . . [T]he arts are. . . viewed
as fundamental ways of knowing the world" (p. 12).
   Another theoretical bias is how I view the abilities of
children. As I worked with and investigated what children are
able to do, I found that the prevailing developmentalist school
of thought, largely influenced by the work of Jean Piaget,
underestimates children's abilities. No research study dealing
with the cognitive abilities of young children can ignore the
work of this giant in the field of child psychology. Jean
Piaget's theories are extremely complex, and therefore difficult
to present briefly without distortion. Instead, I have chosen to

discuss—and criticize—aspects of his theories and work in the chapters where his experiments pertain to the specific topic I am addressing.

It would be a mistake, however, to assume that I disagree with all aspects of Piaget's work. I believe his most important contribution to be his assertion that learning is an *active process*, not a matter of passive absorption; this is a key tenet in which I strongly believe. Piaget also states that children think differently from adults. Again, I agree, although I believe those differences to be quantitative, not qualitative.

My two major disagreements with Piaget's theories are embedded in themes that recur throughout this book. First, his view of learning is more solitary than mine. Piaget believes, for instance, that adults play a minor role in a child's development until he or she is around six or seven years old. I believe, on the other hand, that even much younger children are both intrigued and strongly influenced by the adult world that surrounds them. Secondly, my work with young children has convinced me that they are not as intellectually limited as Piaget claimed; I find them to be neither illogical nor egocentric. Chapter 1 discusses more fully the world of children, and also explains my methodological bias (which clearly leans toward qualitative, field-based research) and the context and methodology of this research.

The following four chapters, 2 through 5, are the real meat of this book, since they discuss my four main findings. Each of these chapters deals with ways that children create symbols in their writing and their drawing in order to add important dimensions to their communications. Although these four findings are presented in separate chapters, dealing with time, space, movement, and color, in reality these dimensions are difficult to separate from one another. Many of the examples from the children's work could have been placed in more than one chapter, but for the sake of examining each more fully, I have somewhat artificially separated them. Finally, my concluding chapter, Chapter 6, reviews my conclusions, reflects on future areas for study, and, most importantly, discusses the implications of this work on the field of literacy and within our educational system.

chapter one

Revisiting the World of Children: Myths, Metaphors, and New Directions for Research

Once when I was six years old I saw a magnificent picture in a book, called *True Stories from Nature*, about the primeval forest. It was a picture of a boa constrictor in the act of swallowing an animal. Here is a copy of the drawing.

In the book it said: "Boa constrictors swallow their prey whole, without chewing it. After that they are not able to move, and they sleep through the six months that they need for digestion."

I pondered deeply, then, over the adventures of the jungle. And after some work with a colored pencil I succeeded in making my first drawing. My Drawing Number One. It looked like this:

I showed my masterpiece to the grown-ups, and asked them whether the drawing frightened them.

But they answered, "Frighten? Why should anyone be frightened by a hat?"

My drawing was not a picture of a hat. It was a picture of a boa constrictor digesting an elephant. But since the grown-ups were not able to understand it, I made another drawing: I drew the inside of the boa constrictor, so that the grown-ups could see it clearly. They always need to have things explained. My Drawing Number Two looked like this:

The grown-ups' response, this time, was to advise me to lay aside my drawing of boa constrictors, whether from the inside or the outside, and devote myself instead to geography, history, arithmetic, and grammar.   (Saint-Exupéry, 1943, pp. 3–4)

When adults look at the world of children, they are necessarily outsiders examining a land they cannot be a part of. And yet the terrain seems so familiar. "The child is familiar to us, yet strange," Jenks (1982) writes, "he inhabits our world and yet appears to answer to another, he is essentially of ourselves and yet appears to display a different order of being" (p. 7).

In interpreting the behaviors and motives of children, adults are liable to approach the task from their own world views and conceptions; they are often quite *adultcentric*. Consider, for example, psychiatrist Robert Burns's interpretation of a child's drawing (Figure 1–1):

Figure 1–1   Billy's Family Drawing (from Burns and Kaufmann, 1972)

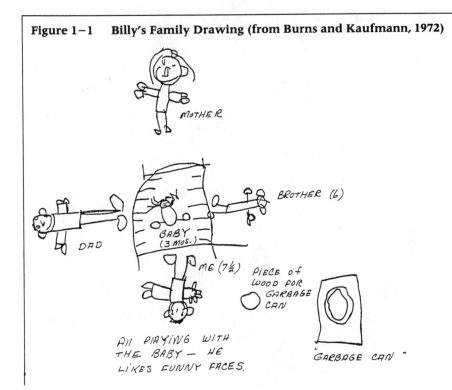

A Baby in the family is an event which usually causes jealousy in other siblings. K-F-D 77 [Figure 1−1] reflects many of the dynamics in the reactions of a child to a new favored baby. This drawing was done by seven-and-one-half-year old Billy, and we note how the baby is the center of the family's attention. Billy is upside down; apparently, this is the way his world is at this time, with a three-month-old baby in the family. We note the crib in which the baby is placed has repetitive lines and some elements of the cross-hatching seen in more obsessive-compulsive cases. In addition, Billy is throwing something in the garbage can. This is a [symbolic] recurrent method of evicting the intruder on the family's peace and quiet. Little children get rid of things in the house that are "nasty" or "dirty" by throwing them in the garbage can. . . . This is a repeated symbol in the new baby syndrome.   (Burns & Kaufman, 1972, p. 174)

Burns and Kaufman are basing their interpretation of Billy's drawing on several assumptions, all coming from the particular symbolic framework in which they are steeped. Even before looking at Billy's drawing, they assume he is jealous and will fit nicely into their preconceived new baby syndrome. And in a very egocentric manner, they assume that Billy is using the two-dimensional space of the page the way they have been conditioned to, and that Billy is, in fact, depicting himself as upside down.

Without asking Billy about the picture and his own in-terpretations, we can't know, of course, what he had in mind, but we can compare his drawing to others. Six-year-old Bobby used space in a similar way in his drawing about playing a new card game when he visited his friend Barry (Figure 1−2).

First he wanted to provide a context for his readers. "That's the T.V. That's one of Barry's robotic things. That's the couch and chair— you know, one of those chairs where you lean it back," he explained as he pointed to different objects on the page. "I'm going to need to make more furniture."

His classmate Josh leaned over the picture. "Oh! It's a top view. Is he looking up or down at the cards?"

"At the cards. See, that's the card." Bobby pointed to the rectangle in the center of the card players. "You put some in the middle to get points. You have to have them to face the other people. You put all the cards down but only one partner keeps it down." (Hubbard, 1987, p. 62)

Instead of using a simple vertical plane of top and bottom, ground and sky, as most adults do, Bobby unfolded the scene into, as Josh immediately perceived, a top view. Bobby does not feel his world is upside down because he is playing a card

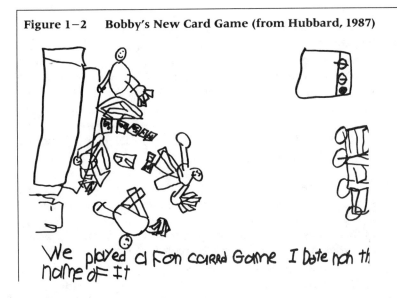

Figure 1–2   Bobby's New Card Game (from Hubbard, 1987)

We played a Fon carRd GamE I Dote not th name oF It

game! I shudder to think of the interpretation Burns and Kaufman might give to the crossed legs or fists full of cards. Nowhere in their book of drawing interpretations do the voices of the children appear to explain the meanings and intentions in their drawings. Instead, the authors rely exclusively on their own assumptions about the world of childhood and the abilities of children.

Unfortunately, they are not alone. This adultcentric view of children pervades our education system. In general, the world of childhood has been distorted, and researchers and educational theorists have systematically underestimated children's true abilities.

The Social History of Childhood

The traditional and still prevailing concept of childhood is that it is a natural state. Yet the line between childhood and adulthood is culturally drawn, evolving to fit the needs of the community (Goldstone, 1986). As the community changes, the metaphors and myths surrounding childhood shift as well.

Research by Phillipe Aries (1962) and Neil Postman (1981) show that childhood itself is a fairly recent cultural invention, virtually nonexistent in the Middle Ages. Medieval artists, for example, did not depict children; they did not know childhood or attempt to portray it. Their renderings of young subjects do not resemble children as we would view them, but look more like miniature adults. In a typical medieval Bible picture of Jesus speaking with children, he seems to be surrounded by dwarves: their clothes, postures, and facial expressions are those of tiny adults.

In many ways, this child-as-miniature-adult metaphor was a true representation of the concept of children. Until the sixteenth century, children dressed exactly as adults and were a part of the adult society as soon as they could be independent of their nanny or mother. According to Postman, this typically occurred around age seven, and after that, "children worked beside adults, drank in taverns with adults, gambled with adults, went to war with adults, and shared beds with adults. Children and adults played the same games. . . .There were no topics or words or activities from which children were supposed to be shielded" (Meyrowitz, 1985, p. 258). In his history of the family in England, Lawrence Stone (1977) offers more evidence of the lack of separation of the child's world from the adult's: "Children saw deaths and executions, witnessed sexual activities, and often engaged in sex play themselves" (p. 84).

But beginning in the sixteenth century, a new concept of the child, and of childhood, emerged. Aries (1962) traces it to the rise of the middle class. Stone (1977) believes it was first discussed by Renaissance humanists, and Elizabeth Eisenstein (1979) puts forth an intriguing theory that links the invention of childhood with literacy. Whatever the cause, sixteenth-century children became a separate class.

At first children were a source of amusement and relaxation for the adults that surrounded them in the home—cuddly and innocent playthings. The seventeenth-century moralists also discovered childhood, but for them, children were not charming toys; they were creatures of God in need of safe-guard—and reform. The Puritans stressed protecting children from the pollution of life. It was believed that accepting un-questioned parental authority would protect children. Stone

(1977) found a determination to "break the will of the child, and to enforce his utter subjection to the authority of his elders and superiors, and most especially, of his parents" (p. 162). The state of Massachusetts went so far as to make disobedience to parents punishable by death. (Stone assures us that "only a handful of children were actually executed under this law" [p. 175].)

This concept of the child quickly merged with the attitudes of the family and melded into the dominant view of the innocent child in need of protection and moral authority—a concept that has influenced the education of children from the seventeenth century. Geoffrey Summerfield (1984) traces the first influential book on the rearing and education of young people to philosopher John Locke's *Some Thoughts Concerning Education* ([1693] 1968). Among other things, Locke recommended that young children, with "all their innocent Folly, Playing, and Childish Actions, are to be left perfectly free and unrestrained, as far as they can consist with Respect to those that are present" (p. 156). These thoughts influenced later Western writers and philosophers, notably Wordsworth (*The Prelude*, 1805), William Blake (*Songs of Innocence and Experience*, 1789), and even Rousseau (*Emile*, 1792), a philosopher who disagreed with Locke on many points, but, according to Summerfield, did not escape his philosophical influence. Cherish children for their own sake is the message of these works; protect their innocence and uniqueness without contaminating them with adult biases.

A complete review tracing the view of the child in educational theory is beyond the scope of this book, but what emerges from the remnants of this philosophy is the image of the child as redeemer. Robert Coles (1986) would like to view children as moral protagonists. Rather than respecting their reasonableness, he instead admires their innate goodness in the tradition of Locke and Wordsworth. Seen in this light, children are expected, according to Madeleine Grumet (1986), to lead and heal our troubled world; they are a special class bearing the burden of saving the universe. The child's "education brings him from sentimental kindergartens and authoritarian classrooms to sun-dappled commencements where we exhort him to make the world a better place" (p. 91). Literature is also replete with examples of the "child as redeemer" theme. One example Grumet gives is Bernard Wishy, who "portrays the child redeemer as an innocent figure who emerged from the rubble of the Civil War to save Americans from the pluralism of urban industrial life. He points to Huck Finn as the child redeemer par excellence, menaced by civilization, fighting to resist its evil lures by escaping to the river" (p. 90). Many believe that this theme, however, is a distortion of what childhood is. One such critic is James Axtell (1976). In his account of education, he discusses the "child redeemer [who] has become the adorable symbol of society's self-deception, a means of foisting the mission of our own liberation upon those least able to effect it" (p. 54).

This brief history shows how our current understanding of children rests on a network of undefended assumptions. William Kessen (1979) reminds us that childhood is, after all, "essentially and eternally a cultural invention" (p. 815).

Reassessing Children's Strengths

Children are typically assessed in terms of what they cannot yet do. In child psychology and development theory, children are viewed as deficient or, at least, incomplete (Speier, 1976). The prevailing metaphor is that of growth: vines and plants growing, buds not yet ready to bloom. "Childhood finds voice only as a distant echo of what is yet to come" (Jenks, 1982, p. 14). This isn't surprising; none other than Charles Darwin is considered to be the godfather of child psychology (Kessen, 1979), followed by G. Stanley Hall and Arnold Gesell, who constantly tied cognitive development to the biological growth of children. In the twentieth century, major figures in child psychology like Piaget, Kagan, and Bruner have worked from a developmental model, plotting the different stages through which children pass on their way to adulthood. They believe that there are qualitative differences between the cognitive abilities of children and adults. Piaget has probably been the most influential, with his central belief in the egocentrism of children, which he feels interferes with their ability to successfully negotiate the world.

In the last decade, many researchers have begun to challenge these notions about children's abilities. Psychologists Sheldon and Barbara White (1980) attack the notion of age-related developmental stages. They suggest that Piaget's age-related cognitive stages are the weakest part of his theory. Since most of these studies are not longitudinal, children are not compared with themselves at a later age. For example, children at age five might be compared to children who are nine years old now. There is no evidence that in four years, these five-year-olds will respond the way the nine-year-olds do now, nor that these nine-year-olds would have responded as today's five-year-olds four years ago.

Marilyn Shatz (1977) is another researcher who finds different stages of thinking for different ages simplistic. Instead, she looks for similarities in the thinking of people at different ages and has found that children seem to vary in their mastery of a skill depending on the nature of the situation.

Margaret Donaldson (1978), in her award-winning book *Children's Minds*, also refutes many aspects of Piaget's theories. She found that when tasks were presented to children within meaningful contexts, they were able to accomplish the same Piagetian tasks they traditionally failed to perform in experimental situations. (See also Black, 1981; Hughes & Grieve, 1979; and McGarrigle & Donaldson, 1974.)

Paul Light (1979) builds on the work of Donaldson and her colleagues. He challenges Piaget's belief in the egocentrism of children. In an interesting series of experiments concerning children's abilities to empathize and play another's part in a situation, he finds that a child's growing social sensitivity is at the core of his or her development. For Light, role-taking rather than egocentrism is that "concept which bridges social and individual aspects of cognition" (p. 117).

These studies show the changing perceptions of the abilities of young children, but the world of infant psychology is changing as well. Daniel Stern (1985) contends that infants are not nearly as passive as has been previously believed. In a longitudinal study where he videotaped the interactions between parents and infants, and later the same parents with these children, he found that the infants had taught their parents to adjust to the degree of stimulation they (the infants) needed. For example, one infant had a more passive temperament than her mother and would break eye contact when in danger of being overstimulated. She also developed other patterns of behavior to train the mother to slow down— patterns that remained intact over the years. On the other hand, eager, active babies found ways to stimulate too-passive mothers and fathers.

Infant specialist Dr. T. Berry Brazelton has also begun to take another look at videotaped interactions between parents and children and to reinterpret the behavior on the tapes. "We used to see the parents shaping the child," he states, "but now we see the child also helping to shape the parents" (quoted in Freidrich, 1983, p. 57).

Unfortunately, not enough researchers have been willing to take another look at the capabilities of children. Too many are like Burns and Kaufman, trapped within their mental framework and unable to break out. Dr. Rochel Gelman (1981) wrote that she and many of her colleagues were blind for many years to the evidence of preschoolers' cognitive and social abilities because they were unwilling to "recognize facts that contradict existing theories" (p. 161).

Consider the research of Howard Gardner (1982), for example, a leading cognitive psychologist working with Project Zero at Harvard University. He consistently designs experimental tasks to test children's artistic concepts, but all the tasks are from his pre-existing developmental framework. He asks children standard sets of questions, never taking into account Donaldson's work, which realizes that a child, in trying to make sense of the situation, may be pondering, What does this adult want? Why is he asking me this?

One of Gardner's (1982) conclusions is that children don't have a sense of an artist's style. In an experiment he conducted, children were shown two paintings—a traditional, realistic painting of a horse by Goya and an abstract Kandinski. He then asked the children if the two paintings could have been painted by the same man. Most said yes, although some reasoned, "No, because he'd be too tired after painting the first one." If I had been one of the children and had never seen the works of either artist before, I might make the same judgment. Artists *do*, after all, change their styles; what if Gardner had chosen instead two Picassos—one from his very early realistic phase and another from his cubist period?

And, in fact, researchers who observe children in a classroom setting as they draw for their own purposes in meaningful contexts have evidence that the children *can* recognize artistic style. Patricia McLure (1987) notes that the six-year-old children in her class recognize and comment on the distinct styles of the other children in the classroom. They also recognize the works of adult artists they are familiar with—picturebook illustrators like Frank Asch, Steven Kellogg, and Trina Schart Hyman. One morning, for example, as Ms. McLure read from E. B. White's *Charlotte's Web*, Roger commented that the pictures were done by Garth Williams, who had illustrated another class favorite—*The Chick Story*. And after the chapter had been read, Barry brought it up again: "I think the background looks like *Stuart Little*. Did Garth Williams illustrate that, too?" (Hubbard, 1985a, p. 157).

Gardner's work is also fraught with the phrase "children cannot yet...." For example, he claims that children in the pre-operational stage cannot manipulate mental images (Gardner, 1982). Yet Allan Paivio (1983) proved that children can rotate things they are familiar with, such as letters, in their minds effortlessly. (See also Chapter 3, "Coping with Flatland.")

The point of this criticism is to highlight the drawbacks of too-narrow assumptions about children and their abilities, drawbacks I hope to avoid, and this calls for a new research methodology, as well as a new metaphor, for children.

The Child as Ethnographic Informant

Bernstein (1983) writes, "Method is not innocent or neutral. It not only presupposes an understanding of what constitutes social and political life; it has also become a powerful factor in shaping (or rather misshaping) human life in the modern world" (p. 45). This has been the case until recently with educational research, a field that has been dominated by positivist traditions. But many researchers are finding this world view getting in the way of a full understanding of human behavior and, especially, human potential. Ton Beekman (1986) declares that "positivism is dead," while Lous Heshesius (1986) provides a bibliography of the accounts of the dissatisfaction in science, philosophy, education, social science, and psychology with the positivistic tradition. A methodological shift is underway, from the quantitative research of the past to a more holistic view. This shift is not necessarily a graceful one, sometimes even occurring in the midst of a study.

Jerome Harste and his colleagues (1984) at Indiana University, for example, began a study of young children who were acquiring written language. Although the Harste group began the study under an experimental framework, it became more and more naturalistic. A sensible compromise appeared to be to meld the two designs, which the researchers attempted but soon abandoned, reasoning that the two methods ultimately represented different and incompatible world views. Their tasks became more and more open-ended, and they came to view the children as their "curricular informants," showing the researchers the process of their learning (Harste & Rowe, 1986).

More and more educational researchers are making similar shifts, researchers like James Britton, Kenneth and Yetta Goodman, Donald Graves, Jane Hansen, Don Holdaway, and Frank Smith. But I propose an even more radical step: to study the world of children anthropologically. This method would view the world of children as its own culture and expand Harste's metaphor so that children can teach us as *ethnographic informants.*

Ethnography is the work of describing a culture. Malinowski (1922) explains that the goal is "to grasp the native's point of view, his relation to life, to realize *his* vision of *his* world" (p. 25). And the way the ethnographer learns this culture is through his or her informant, a native speaker who acts as a source of information. The informant literally becomes the ethnographer's teacher. If we invite children to become our ethnographic informants, we can begin to understand their world on their terms, without falling prey to pre-existing assumptions about their abilities. In this new role, the child is not the passive subject of the research, but an active collaborator.

When we shift to an ethnographic perspective, another fundamental difference is implied. In traditional research, the unit of study is the single child, in keeping with the still prevailing Piagetian notion of the individual child constructing and reinventing concepts within her world. Some psychologists, such as William Kessen (1979), argue that this is a difficult model to escape because it is the core of our American culture: "The child—like the Pilgrim, the cowboy, the detective on television—is invariably seen as a freestanding isolable being who moves through development as a self-contained and complete individual" (p. 819). Ethnographic research, on the other hand, with its emphasis on the wider culture takes seriously the notion that development is largely a social construction. (Researchers like Paul Light, 1979, Lev Vygotsky, 1978, and Berger & Luckmann, 1966, stress this notion.)

In reviewing the ethnographic literature, I found that anthropologists have indeed relied on children as informants in the past. James Spradley (1979), for example, who has studied cultures as diverse as Skid Row and cocktail lounges, recalls Laurie, a kindergarten student, as one of his best informants. "She answered my questions with the calm assurance of an expert. She recalled incidents that had happened and told me stories that brought to life the cultural scene she knew so well. It didn't matter that she had just passed her fourth birthday; she had mastered the complex culture of her kindergarten class" (p. 26).

Ton Beekman (1986) is another researcher who "stepped inside the landscape of the child" (p. 39) to find out more about the child's world. As a clinical psychologist from the Netherlands, she had been studying children's experiences of time and space but found the research limited. She writes, "We read the literature about these issues, but the emphasis there was only on the cognitive aspects of the children's experiences. In the standard texts, we can discover all the things children still don't know, and what adult-defined developmental stage they are in. But as phenomenologists, we realize that in order to understand children's experiences, we need to observe them directly, not through the myopic lenses of our adult-centered theories" (p. 41). Beekman and her associates found that the best way to discover the time and space experiences of the Netherlands children was to enter their world, joining them in their daily games of hide-and-seek.

There are, of course, stumbling blocks in opening up the ethnographer-informant relationship. Typically, adults hold a position of authority over children, so even innocent questions might be interpreted as requiring deferential answers. But adults can show children by joining in their routines and by an attitude of genuine respect that they truly do want to be accepted and learn from their child informants. Researcher William Corsaro (1981) found that he was referred to as "that big kid—he has to go school, too," and "Big Bill" (p. 117). In my own work in a first grade, I knew I had been accepted as a somewhat bigger classmate when six-year-old Noa called me up to invite me over to play one afternoon.

Above all, this type of research requires time and the patience to learn the recipes of behavior that guide the culture of the children we are studying. Looking at the symbol systems that the children create as they learn to read and write means learning to see *"their* vision from *their* point of view"* (Malinowski, 1922, p. 25). For it is only from the perspective of the children themselves that we can learn to see the elephants inside boa constrictors rather than ordinary hats.

Ethnographic Context and Population

Mast Way School, in Lee, New Hampshire, is a small elementary school, with children from kindergarten through grade five. The backgrounds of the children's parents range from blue-collar and farming families to professionals, with the majority of the children coming from middle- and upper-middle-class families. Several years ago, this school was the site of a reading and writing project conducted by a state university team. As a researcher on that team, I spent eighteen months in one of the first-grade classrooms working collaboratively with the teacher, Patricia McLure. Our history of working together, as well as my familiarity with the classroom context, led me to return to this site. The class I researched was one of three first grades, all heterogeneously grouped. It began with twenty-one students and grew to twenty-four, eleven boys and thirteen girls, by December. (The names of the Mast Way Elementary School and the teacher, Patricia McLure, are not pseudonyms but are used with Ms. McLure's and the school principal's permission. All other names pertaining to this classroom and any children's names used throughout the text are pseudonyms, however, in accordance with requirements set by the University of New Hampshire Human Subjects Review Board.)

Figure 1–3   Pat McLure's First-Grade Classroom

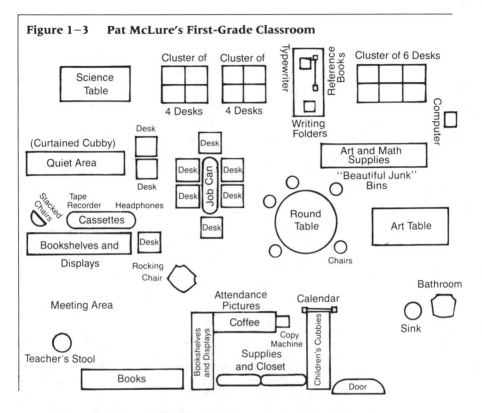

Patricia McLure's classroom had the atmosphere of a productive studio workshop. When the six-year-olds entered her classroom at 8:35 in the morning, they went directly to their writing folders. They chose what they wished to write about, what type of paper they would use, and where they wished to write. There were various places to sit and work—long tables, round tables, desks in clusters, and individual desks the children could move together. At the front of the room was a large carpeted meeting area, bordered by a well-stocked class library (Figure 1–3).

Plants and microscopes, scales and weights, polliwogs and seashells—every available shelf and wall space beckoned to be explored. Stacks of paper, single sheets, and stapled booklets were available, as well as a variety of writing utensils and other art supplies; the Beautiful Junk bin overflowed with scrap materials ranging from pieces of cloth to leftover wrapping paper. The walls were covered with the children's experiments, notes, projects, graphs, and artwork.

The following table summarizes the morning time frame in the class:

8:35–9:10	"Writing Time"
9:10–9:30	Whole-Group Share (Writing)
9:30–10:00	"Working Time" (Usually reading, and often a choice of math or reading or another activity, such as graphs or journals.)
10:00–10:15	Snack
10:15–10:30	Recess
10:30–10:45	Whole-Group Share (Reading)
10:45–11:15	"Working Time" (Similar to first—reading-sharing groups, math, other work projects.)

A full discussion of the classroom context as well as a detailed look at the different components of the children's morning appears in the appendix.

Field Entry and Data Collection

Beginning on the first day of school, I was a member of the first-grade community for three mornings a week—Monday, Tuesday, and Thursday—from approximately 8:00 to 11:15 A.M. For four months, September through December, I adhered to this schedule. In January, I began to withdraw from the field, spending one morning a week in the classroom instead of three. The main data gathering, then, covered a four-month period, and the remaining two served to confirm patterns that had emerged in the data and to remain in contact with the members of the classroom community.

I followed a fairly regular routine. During the morning, I read and wrote with the children and circulated around the room talking with them about the pieces they were reading or writing, and interviewing them about their composing processes. I also audio-taped conversations that children had among themselves and with me, as well as the daily whole-group writing and reading share sessions. And each day, I sketched the classroom setup, documenting where and with whom the children chose to work during both writing and reading, taking special note of the five children in the class with whom I spent the most time, my nisbas.

The Nisbas

Wayne Booth (1974) proposes that we revise our Western notions about the isolated individual:

What happens, then, if we choose to begin with our knowledge that we are essentially creatures made in symbolic interchange, created in the process of sharing intentions, values, meanings; in fact, more like each other than different, more valuable in our commonality than in our idiosyncrasies: not, in fact, anything at all when considered separately from our relations? What happens if we think of ourselves as essentially participants in a field or process or mode of *being persons together?* (p. 134)

Karen LeFevre (1987) suggests we need to reconceptualize "the self as a social entity"; and Gregory Bateson (1972) describes a "self not bounded by skin but interacting constantly with the environment." To move beyond the "isolated individual" as a unit of study, I chose to borrow a term from Geertz's (1983) work and study five *nisbas* in the social context of their classroom.

Anthropologist Clifford Geertz (1983) describes how Moroccans refer to a person not with a unique name, but instead with a *nisba*—a term that changes to show that person's relation to certain social groups or contexts. The nisba is incorporated into the personal name by adding *i* (male) or *iya* (female). (For example, *Susi* is a man coming from the region *Sus; hrari* is a silk merchant, or one who sells *hrar,* silk.) Geertz claims that the use of the nisba suggests a different understanding of the individual, where persons are not regarded as "bounded psychic entities detached from their backgrounds and singularly named, [but rather as] selves that gain their definition from associative relations they...have with the society that surrounds them. They are contextualized persons" (p. 66). (The coining of this term is a good example of "invention as a social act." I am indebted to Brenda Miller for suggesting this name for the concept. She, in turn, claims to be indebted to Karen LeFevre's discussion of the term *nisba* in *Invention as a Social Act,* 1987.)

I modified this Moroccan term, using it to describe "contextualized persons." Although I did select five children to look at more closely, I did not examine them as typical case studies. Rather than being described as individuals in separate chapters, they appear as examples throughout the book. Their processes are reported in the context in which they occurred, against the backdrop of the first-grade classroom culture. And, although I spent more time with these particular children, I also interviewed, observed, and interacted with all the children, so the whole class is represented within the study.

The five children I chose as nisbas were very different from one another, both in their literacy strategies and in their social roles within the classroom. They were alike in their willingness to talk with me and to share their work in progress and their strategies for making meaning. Kelly was the first child I chose. I noticed her interest in combining pictures and print in her early writing booklets. From the first day of school, she kept up a running protocol of her process as she worked. A bright, affectionate girl, I soon learned that she had a "whim of iron," and if I were not immediately available when she wanted to share something with me, the incident was not soon forgotten.

Her strategies were clearly different from Paul's: his first booklets had few drawings and were full of carefully printed letters and words. My original hypothesis—that words could communicate his meaning best—proved to be way off base. Instead, he eventually described vivid memories and mental images to me that he did attempt to capture through pictures, but his perfectionist tendencies often got in the way. "When I put the pictures on paper, they're not like in my head," he complained.

Ming was one of the social stars of the classroom, always knowing how to capture the attention of her neighbors with just the right story about "yucky dog biscuits my brother eats" or intriguing references to her arrival in America from Korea. Adept at reading social situations, she would gauge her audience's reactions carefully at whole-class share sessions to judge what kinds of topics and storytelling methods would continue to bring approval.

There's a child like Graham in most clases—a bright, verbal little boy in a perpetual state of disorganization. His writing at the beginning of the year tended to be a lot of motion and movement acted out as it happened on the page—tales of Ghostbusters and Transformers with little story line but lots of action! I chose Graham because teachers often ask about the processes and progress of such a child.

And for my final nisba, I settled on Claudia, an orphan from Portugal who had been adopted only a few months earlier and was still learning the basics of a new language, culture, and climate. She initially coped with the demands of writing time by using clues from the classroom environment, carefully copying words like "red crayon," "Mrs. McLure," and letters of the alphabet with their corresponding pictures from the illustrated alphabets around the room.

Over the next few months, these children shared their learning processes with me. Through the samples of their work, the stories from their classroom, and the transcripts of their conversations, I hope readers of this book will come to know these children—not in isolation but as contextualized persons. They are the guides who helped to show me the visual and verbal systems that children create to communicate the important dimensions of time, space, movement, and color.

chapter two

Signs
of the Times

*What, then, is time? If no one asks me, I know: if I wish to
explain to one that asketh, I know not.*
Augustine

One of the ways we order our existence is to mark time segments. We remember the past, observe the present, and anticipate the future. And we use the symbols of time in our everyday speech and actions. But, as sociologist Michael Flaherty (1987) points out, "Our clocks mark time, but they do not make time" (p. 313).

Children's Concepts of Time

We think of children as coming into the world with a sense of time, yet the development of time perception is actually an adaptive process—one that is culturally developed. Although we know that infants are affected by the tempo-rhythms around them (Akhundov, 1986), it is still difficult to study time perception because we have no sense organ for perceiving time: we hear with our ears and see with our eyes, but there is no sense organ for time perception (Fraser, 1975).

Perhaps because of this inherent difficulty, children's conceptions of time have largely been ignored, even by the leading child psychologists and child development specialists. Jerome Kagan's *The Nature of the Child* (1984) does not even mention time concepts. And the idea of time is little more than a footnote for both Margaret Donaldson (1978) and Lev Vygotsky (1978). Both look at time only in relation to print—concluding that making meaning permanent through writing can help develop a child's sense of past and future.

Only Jean Piaget (1945) was brave enough to attempt to study that fourth dimension and children's understanding of it. Piaget believed that time could only be studied in relation to velocity: "The hypothesis I should like to defend is that, psychologically, time depends on velocity" (p. 202). From this point, he went on to ask the question "How does the child arrive at the idea of velocity?" (p. 203). Basing his results on a series of experiments with young children, Piaget concluded that children are not able to have a concept of time until they are able to conserve velocity. The pre-operational child will imagine that when he begins to run, the clock goes more slowly than he does, or that when he walks, the clock goes faster. (The terms *conserve* and *pre-operational* are both important aspects of Piagetian developmental theory. For a concise explanation of Piaget's developmental stages, see the helpful appendix in Margaret Donaldson's *Children's Minds* [1978]. For a clear explanation of Piaget's cognitive theories, see B. Wadsworth, *Piaget's Theory of Cognitive and Affective Development* [1984].)

Although I believe we owe a great debt to Piaget for tackling difficult issues in child psychology, I find several problems with this pioneer work in children's concepts of time. First, the experiments themselves have the same problems of validity that recent researchers have found in other areas of Piaget's work (see Chapter 1, "Revisiting the World of Children"). Consider this example of one of Piaget's (1945) experiments to study a child's logical concepts of time:

To study this is a simple matter. One uses the flow of water from a pyriform glass into a cylindrical glass placed beneath the first one. The child will have to reconstruct the order of events by ordering a series of cards showing the levels of water at different stages of flow. In addition, we ask the child whether the time that has passed is the same, or greater, or less, than that between two other given stages. Thus the task is a problem of classification of the intervals posed before any measurement of time can take place.   (p. 215)

There is no reason to believe that this task makes sense to children—that they understand what it is they are to do and why. As with some of the other Piagetian experiments, Donaldson (1978) and her colleagues argue that "there is no play of interpersonal motives of such a kind as to make it instantly intelligible....There is the question of the experimenter's motives in asking the child to do it and the child's motives in responding" (p. 17).

Another difficulty underlying Piaget's studies in this area is his definition of time. He argues that all time can be tied to an understanding of velocity, but I find this concept quite narrow. What about the phenomena of different experiences with *lived time*, for example? We are all familiar with days that drag on, each minute seeming interminable, or vacations where weeks seem like hours, or concepts of the future or past that can hardly be fit into Piaget's neat mathematical formula, "according to which time equals work divided by power" (p. 212).

But to me, the most troublesome of Piaget's ideas of time conception is his assumption that the principles of Western logic, Western mathematics, *and* Western concept of time are universals. There is a strong body of research that demonstrates that concepts of time are not natural, but culturally tied. Although Piaget—and most Europeans and North Americans—tend to think of time as something fixed in nature and very linear, other cultures view it quite differently.

Edward Hall (1983) explains the great differences between "white time" and "Hopi time." Some of the differences are fundamental and immediately recognizable: for whites, time is a noun; for the Hopi, time is a verb. Other differences are more subtle: "white time allows for loss of collective memory; Hopi time does not" (p. 12). Hall shows how these differences completely ruined the building of a government-sponsored dam.

In Southern Asia, the view of the future is quite different from our concept of future: while we think of the foreseeable future, the Eastern concept involves centuries. According to Hall (1959), they would think it quite realistic to think of "a long time" in terms of thousands of years, or even an endless period. At the opposite extreme are the Navajo, where the present is of utmost importance and the future has little reality attached to it.

Besides length of time, other concepts can have quite an effect. Imagine the difficulties of living on Truk (in the Southwest Pacific) where time does not heal. Disputes and disagreements that occurred years ago are treated as if they just happened—they stack up and weigh on the present (Hall, 1959).

American time has its own special cultural aspects. "As a rule, Americans tend to think of time as a road or a ribbon stretching into the future, along which one progresses. The road has segments or compartments [that] are to be kept discrete" (Hall, 1959, p. 7). But this is only one aspect of our concept of time—the linear end of what Stephen Jay Gould (1987) calls our "crucial dichotomy" (p. 10). He contends that while on the one hand we have "time's arrow"—with every moment part of an irreversible sequence of events—on the other hand we have "time's cycle"—"apparent motions are parts of repeating cycles, and differences of the past will be realities of the future" (p. 11).

Children in our American culture learn these two important concepts of time. But if they are not born with a particular time perception hard-wired in and aren't developmentally progressing toward a cognitive time universal, how *do* they acquire our concept of time? I believe that children actively construct a social world around them, using their growing mastery of language—and of interactional strategies—to become socialized to the cultural world of which they are a part. (For purposes of this book, I will use Cook-Gumperz's definition of socialization as "the growth of social understanding and of the capabilities for the maintenance of social relations that develop throughout childhood"—1986, p. 42.) And since time's arrow and time's cycle are integral parts of children's social world, they work hard to understand them. I see evidence of their struggles in the signs and symbols they create to depict both these concepts of time.

Time's Arrow

Children construct many kinds of symbols as they work out the linear progression of time the adults around them use regularly and take for granted.

Early in the year, Kelly used a combination of print and pictures to get across the concept of passing time (Figure 2−1). The words in her story hint at the passage of time: "The Mississippi River in a storm" (Figure 2−1, B) places the time as in the present, and "A Mississippi River boat docks after a storm" (Figure 2−1, C) uses the linguistic time marker "after." But Kelly has created a more powerful symbol to show the sequence of events through her drawing itself. She uses the black of the coming and going storm quite consciously to reinforce and extend the words she has written. And when she explained her story to me, she began with the present, then worked backward and forward.

"You see, the steamboat here [Figure 2−1, B] is *in* the storm," she began. "This is the water coming down here. On the page before [Figure 2−1, A], you can see, the storm is just coming. I'll make the black on the other side now, going away to show the storm is going away [Figure 2−1, C]."

Figure 2–1   Kelly's Steamboat

the
Mississippi
river,

a

the Mississippi
river in p st
orom.

b

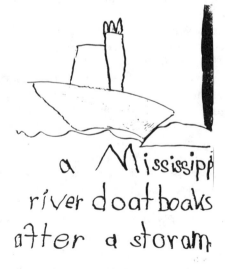

a Mississippi
river doatboaks
after a storam

c

Figure 2–2   Eugene's Cocoon

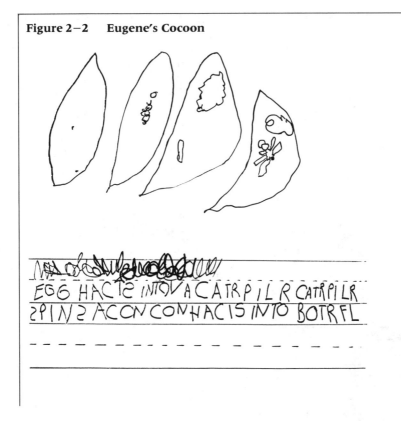

EGG HACTE INTOV A CATRPILR CATRPILR
ZPINZ ACCN CONHACIS INTO BOTRFL

Eugene used a very different system to show the progression of time (Figure 2–2). In his story about butterflies, he used a kind of time line to show the sequence of events. Once again, the words and pictures work together to show the four stages Eugene wanted to demonstrate: there's the egg (at left in Figure 2–2) that hatches into a caterpillar (second from left); then the caterpillar spins a cocoon (third from left) and finally, the cocoon hatches into a butterfly (at right). Just as in Kelly's story, Eugene's words and pictures need to reinforce each other; neither could really stand alone and depict what the author had in mind.

Megan used an established convention—word bubbles with small circles—to denote thought, but she used them in an interesting way to show future events in her dog story.

And once again, she needed verbal markers to make it clear to her audience that she is giving an added dimension to her word bubbles (Figure 2−3).

One page of her story is in the present: "K. K. *is buying* a

Figure 2−3   Megan's Dog Story

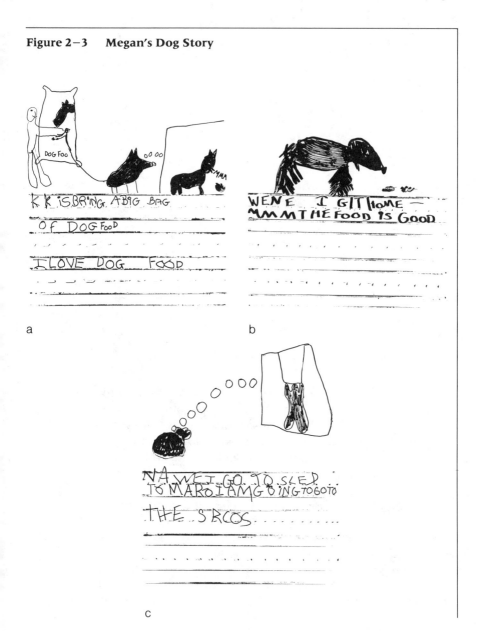

a

b

c

bag of dog food" (Figure 2–3, A; emphasis mine). The dog is imagining the future by picturing himself there in his thoughts. And Megan doesn't leave it to chance that we will figure out her use of this convention. On the next page of her story, she reinforces it linguistically: "When I get home, 'Mmmm' the food is good." The future has come to pass (Figure 2–3, B). And later in the story, she again uses the thought bubble convention with the time markers "now" and "tomorrow," making it clear that once again, the dog is projecting himself into the future: "Now I go to sleep. Tomorrow I am going to go to the circus" (Figure 2–3, C).

Some children rely almost exclusively on linguistic symbols to note the sequence of events and the linear progression of time. Paul's writing is full of markers like "tomorrow," "before," and especially "We are going to." In his Cub Scout story, for example, he carefully recorded the sequence of events in his weekly scout meetings, reflecting on past, present, and future (Figure 2–4). He remembered the Halloween party and what everyone wore, he placed himself firmly in the present as a current scout member (Figure 2–4, A): "I go to Tiger Scouts." And he projected to future events (Figure 2–4, B): "In the winter time we are going to go sledding."

The electronic media also affected Paul's use of time symbols, as his organization in the nonfiction T.V. story shows (see Figure 2–5). The first part of his story is about "good food": "Carrots are good for you and I like them. Yum. Yum" (Figure 2–5, A). The next page (Figure 2–5, B) continued this story in the top half of the page, with the picture of a potato, captioned "A potato in the ground." But just like a

---

Figure 2–4   Paul's Tiger Cub Writing

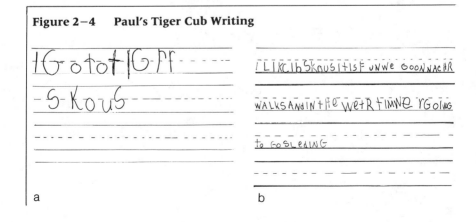

a   b

television announcer, Peter warned the reader that the story would be interrupted by an important message: "After this message, we'll be right back." The important message? "Eight more days until Christmas" (Figure 2−5, C). Then, just as at the end of a commercial, Paul continued with the main story: "Now we'll return to 'Good Food,'" he began. The story continued, "But candy is bad for you" (Figure 2−5, D). As Paul's T.V. story continues, it follows the time markers he sees on television, switching back between his three main stories— "Good Food," "Dinosaurs," and "Space," and important messages and announcements, like the amount of time left until Christmas and the latest-breaking local news of a bus crash (See Figures 2−5, E−H).

Figure 2−5   Paul's TV Story

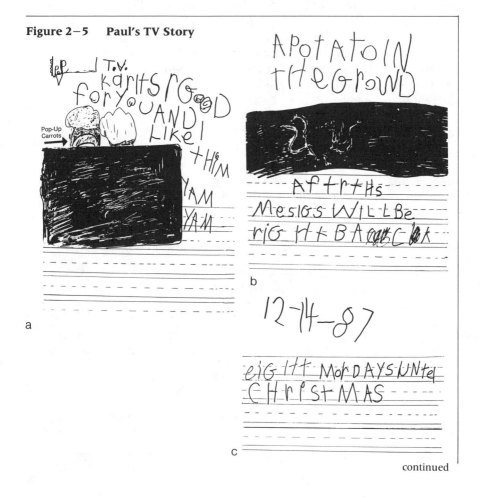

continued

Figure 2–5   Continued

BUT CANDY IS BAD for you

NoW We Wel Lrytern IS ooDFooD

d

CUMING UP Next IS THe NeWPs e Wer

e

AND I LIKe BeyNs

f

THe BAD NeWS IS one oF THe BUSes crasht AND IT WISIN Lee

g

ANDoNe OF THe BUSes HADACAr crashlt

h

Figure 2−6 Graham's Clocks

Other children, like Graham, use picture symbols with few linguistic markers to show time progression. Graham used tiny clocks to symbolize the order of events and the amount of time they took the day he and his family went to the Asia restaurant to eat. Again, he starts with the present, then works backward and forward (Figure 2−6).

"I would think it was about that time," he explained to me, pointing to the second clock, "when we were eating, and I would say it was about this time," he continued, pointing to the clock on the previous page, "when we went in." He thought for a minute, drew the third clock, and then re-explained the time sequence, always pointing to the tiny clocks.

"It was about one o'clock, actually, when we went in, and here, it was about six o'clock, and here," Graham pointed to the last scene, "it was about seven o'clock."

Graham's written words alone would not have shown the passage of time—or the breakdown of time segments—that he had in mind. So he relied on an accepted cultural symbol to show that linear progression. But that linear arrow of time is not the only symbol in the children's writing and drawing; there is also the cycle of time.

Time's Cycle

The sun also ariseth, and the sun goeth down, and hasteth to his place where he arose....The thing that hath been, it is what shall be; and that which is done is that which shall be done.
                                                    (Ecclesiastes 1:5 and 1:9)

Although the notion of the cyclical nature of time, as expressed in this biblical passage, is not a dominant one in our culture, it is nevertheless a deeply embedded one, and an important aspect of the Western concept of time that young children come to terms with.

Very early in the year, I began to notice examples of writing and drawing about the seasons. Many of these books were not limited to only one season. The importance of these stories was in the inclusion of *each* season, in the correct order. One of Ming's first writing topics was a season book, where she depicted winter, spring, summer, and fall, each with an activity symbol of that time of year. On her first page, she wrote about winter: "The kids is going outside to play in the snow." But the rest of the book is more clearly a labeled concept book. "Summer time," she wrote under a picture of herself catching butterflies (Figure 2−7, A) and for "Fall time" (Figure 2−7, B), she is jumping in a pile of leaves.

Figure 2−7   Ming's Season Book. A: Summer Time. B: Fall Time.

Figure 2-8   Sarah's Book "Sizinse" (Seasons). A: Winter. B: Spring.

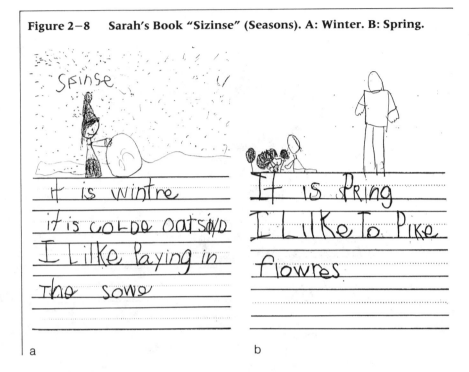

a   b

Sarah also begins with winter in her book entitled "Seasons" (Figure 2-8). In this book, she too places herself within the activities of the season she is writing about. And although the book is meant to span the entire year, these activities are always placed in the present tense. To project herself into that past or future time, the pictures are not enough; she needs the words as well. In winter, for example (Figure 2-8, A), Sarah writes, "I like playing in the snow," while in spring (Figure 2-8, B), "I like to pick flowers." And each of her statements about an activity is prefaced with a marker of a season: "It is winter," for example, or "It is spring."

In October, when gardens were frosting over and flowers were dying, some children in Pat McLure's class reflected on the cyclical nature of plant life. It was during this time that Linda wrote a story called "My Rose" (see Figure 2-9) and shared it with the class. In her book, the flower dies, yet on the next page, it's "all better."

Figure 2−9   Linda's Flower

When the children questioned her about this, she was forced to explain what she meant in increasingly clearer terms. First, Sally asked her, "How could it get back to life?" Linda's answer, "The flower is happy because it's raining, and it's happy," had meaning to her, but not to others in the class. Nick refused to leave it at that, and asked again, "But how could your flower die and come alive again?" And this time, they were satisfied with her answer: "'Cause the seeds stay in the ground."

Figure 2−10   Ming's Flower

A few days later, Ming shared *her* dying flower story, which begins and ends with planting seeds (see Figure 2−10). This time, none of the children questioned her about the flower dying and reappearing. In fact, when Susan asked her which part she liked best, Ming replied, "The part where it's dead." Instead of this remark causing any controversy, it sparked a lively discussion about other experiences of flowers dying.

The children also worked out the natural time cycles they observed in the skies. Several children wrote about watching the sun—or "my sun" as Kelly calls it. Claudia wrote about herself and her cat in relation to both the sun and the moon. And when she shared it with the class, the discussion focused on whether it was the sun or the moon. Eugene used the symbol of the harvest moon to indicate both that the season was fall and that, as his text read, "The day is over." When Sarah wrote and drew about the differences between the sun and the moon, she compared what happens to these two heavenly bodies. First, she showed two pages from her story

Figure 2–11   Sarah's Moon and Sun

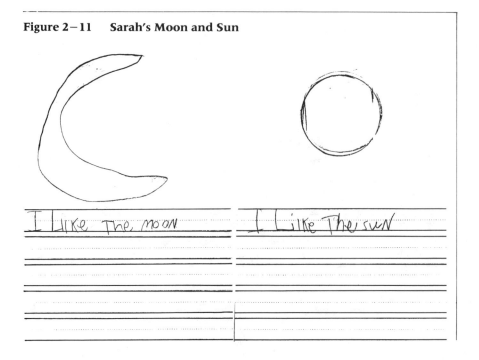

(Figure 2–11). "I went for a star walk with just my Mom. It was real late at night and that made me think about writing about this," she explained. "At the beginning, the moon is kinda thin, and it gets bigger and bigger. One side, like this, is flat sometimes. Then it's almost a full moon, and you hafta wait. Then it comes back."

She turned to her page about the sun. "The sun doesn't change. It just comes up and goes down. Sometimes, I watch the sun go down," she looked up at me and stated emphatically, "but not up!"

The children also wrote and drew about occasions and holidays that return every year. They anticipated certain rituals with these events, like Christmas and Hanukkah. In December, Gwen and Sally talked together as they wrote about the upcoming holidays.

"I'm thinking of all the Christmases," Gwen confided, "but mostly the one that's coming up. I don't know why. I think of Santa and decorations and snow."

Figure 2–12   Kelly's Cake

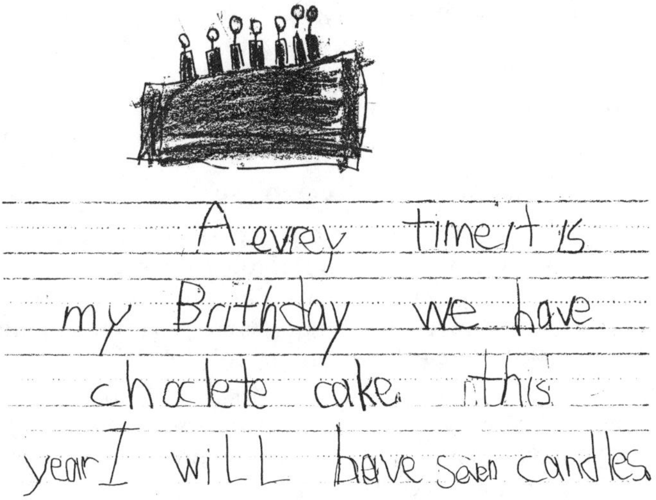

"You're complicating me up." Sally complained. I'm thinking about last year's Hanukkah. We always play dredles, and the first night, we light three candles on the Menorah. I always know it's coming when Christmas is coming."

Birthday traditions are also a part of time's cycle in our culture. Many children, like Kelly, reflect on the recurrence of that yearly celebration—the same each year, but slightly different. "Every time it is my birthday, we have chocolate cake," she wrote. "This year, I will have seven candles" (Figure 2–12).

The Role of the Teacher

The examples I have discussed are all from the writing topics the children chose themselves. But there were other parts of the day, and areas of the curriculum, where their teacher had more say in the topics they wrote about. Often, Pat McLure chose areas to study that helped acculturate the children to both time's arrow and time's cycle. Although the time aspect was not a deliberate component of her curriculum, it is nevertheless implicitly present. I found it most clearly demonstrated in the science assignments and the discussions Pat led. A more conscious goal in her teaching was helping the children learn to understand the time segments of her daily schedule and the connectedness of learning across yesterday, today, and tomorrow. This, in turn, would help them be successful in school beyond the first grade.

Reinforcing Time's Arrow: Rotten Jack

In October, Pat began a long unit on jack-o'-lanterns. One of the components was for the children to each write directions for how to carve a jack-o'-lantern—directions that could be understood by a partner. The children were given the latitude to use a combination of words and pictures to convey these directions. To make their directions work, they learned that it was essential to break the operations into segments, which were to be kept discrete. This exercise is consistent with our cultural view of the necessity of "one thing at a time" (Hall, 1959, p. 6).

The four examples in Figure 2–13 show the range of solutions the children used, with their symbols—both pictorial and written—to complete their directions. Some children, like Nick, relied almost exclusively on the picture. His only other symbols were dashes, numbers, and arrows to show the operations and the order in which to perform them (Figure 2–13, A). Megan's figure is just as prominent in her directions, but the words play a more significant role as she explains her six-step procedure (Figure 2–13, B). Kelly and Debbie both rely more heavily on the print in their papers (Figure 2–13, C and D). Debbie's drawings, in fact, are more for decoration than to actually show *how* to carve the pumpkin.

When the directions were completed and the children had decided on how they wanted Jack carved, the next phase of the unit began. Pat supervised the carving, and then the children were given science journals in which to observe and record the daily changes in Jack—who was soon renamed "Rotten Jack" (see Figure 2–14). The nature of the project seemed to help the children relate past time segments to the present and, ultimately, to the future. Kelly noticed details,

Figure 2–13   **Directions for Carving a Jack-O'-Lantern. A: Nick's Directions. B: Megan's Directions. C: Kelly's Directions. D: Debbie's Directions.**

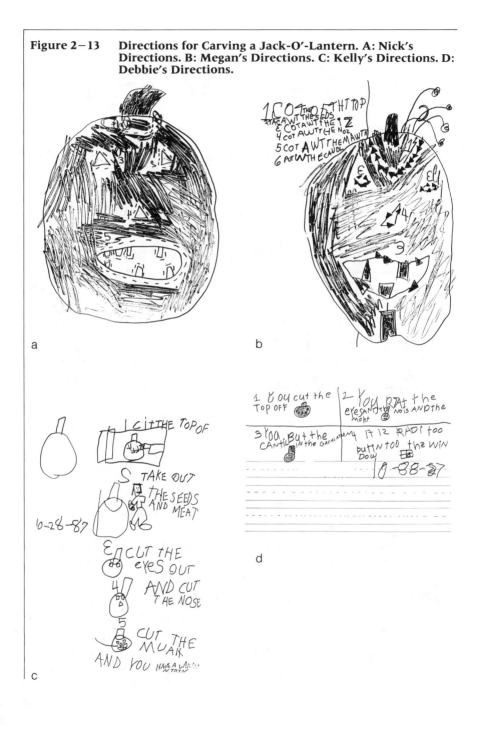

Figure 2–14 Rotten Jack Journals. A: Kelly's. B: Nick's. C: Eugene's. D–E: Megan's. F–G: Graham's.

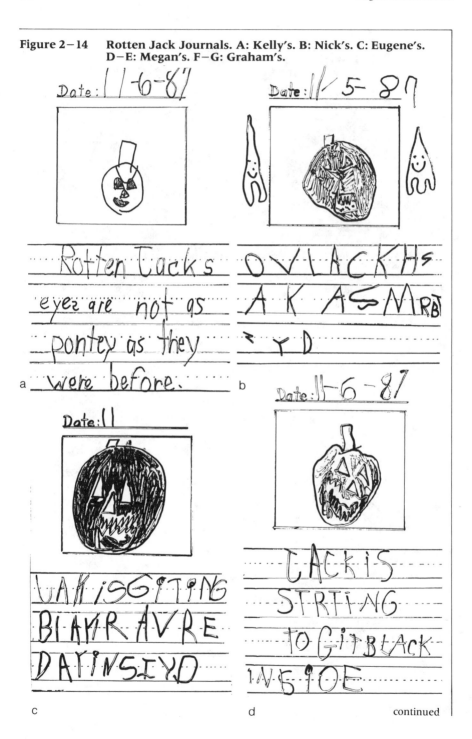

continued

Figure 2–14   Continued

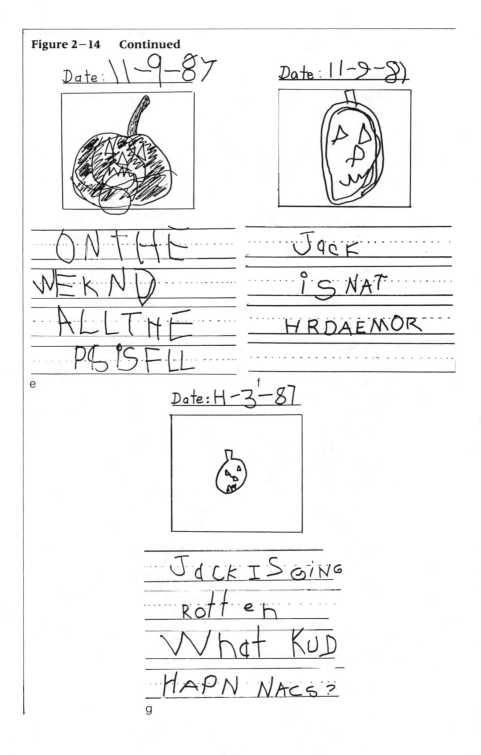

Date: 11-9-87

Date: 11-9-87

ON THE
WEKND
ALLTHE
PSISFLL

e

Jack
IS NAT
HRDAEMOR

Date: H-3-87

f

JdCK IS oiNG
Rotten
What KuD
HAPN NACS?

g

like the changes in his eyes: "Rotten Jack's eyes are not as pointy as they were before" (Figure 2–14, A). Nick focused on some of the bigger changes when he drew a large crack in Rotten Jack and reinforced it with the words "It is much bigger than yesterday" (see Figure 2–14, B). Eugene focused on the color changes: "Jack is getting blacker every day inside" (see Figure 2–14, C).

Megan, too, noticed the color changes in relation to how Jack used to be: "Jack is starting to get black inside" (Figure 2–14, D). But on other days, she needed to write in the past tense to show what happened when she wasn't there: "On the weekend, all the pieces fell" (see Figure 2–14, E). And while most of Graham's observations focused on the present in relation to the past—"Jack is not hard any more" (see Figure 2–14, F)—these observations also helped him project into the future: "Jack is getting rotten. What could happen next?" (Figure 2–14, G).

Hypothesizing about what happened and why, as well as guessing what will happen next, were important components of Pat's Rotten Jack unit. When the project ended abruptly one Monday morning—Jack had gotten so rotten he fell off the shelf over the weekend—Pat expected the children to reflect on what had happened. Their hypotheses needed to be based on what they had seen. When Jimmy guessed, "I think he tripped over hisself," Pat gently corrected him, reminding the children, "We need to think very carefully about this being true information. Just what we've seen." The children *did* think very carefully. They put together the daily changes they had observed and recorded in the past to explain this present event, as this transcript from my field notes (November 9, 1987) shows:

Pat: What has happened to [Rotten Jack]? Eugene?

Eugene: I think that it looks like he got a little too much soft on the inside.

Pat: Um-hm. He did get very soft on the inside.

Nick: I think the top got all squishy and stuff and he collapsed.

Pat: He did collapse. That's true. It was hard to tell. When I came in this morning, and it was on the ground, it was hard to tell what had happened on the top. The stem had broken off from the top.

Claudia: Um, I tink he, I know why the pumpkin fell down.

Pat: Why did the pumpkin fall down?

Claudia: Um, because, um, all brown, and black, and white.

Pat: That's right. And all of that made it very soft.

Claudia: And then it fall down.

Paul: Um, I think maybe the top fell in there, and then it jiggled it so it fell down. And it's just, so, uh, loose, it just fell apart, or maybe, it was the stem that was a little heavy, and the top was so heavy and the sides were so soft that it pushed it down, it was so heavy. . . .

Claudia: I tink, I tink the pumpkin fall down all by itself because he, because the soft stuff move. . . .

Pat: Mmm-hmm. Eugene?

Eugene: I, I, I think Paul's theory that the top fell in, except first I think it might have fallen apart and then fell down.

When the discussion ended, the children wrote their final entries in their science journals. Kelly took Pat's reminder about true observations very much to heart. When I asked her what she thought she would write, she thought she might write about what would happen in the future to Rotten Jack. But, she emphasized, "We could write what we think's gonna happen as long as it really *could* happen. Like, I think he's gonna get thrown out, or I think Mr. Remick is gonna throw him out. . . ." Although Kelly's pumpkin journal is written in the present, she uses it not only to reflect on the past but also to project into the future.

Table 2–1 summarizes the children's uses of time in their Rotten Jack journals. It provides a classwide picture. The most common tense was the present, and all children in the class used this tense on some days. This is not surprising, but what *is* impressive is that more than half the class (twelve out of twenty-two children) used a more complicated verb structure to represent the present in relation to the past. For example, Kelly wrote, "Rotten Jack's eyes are not as pointy as they were before" (Figure 2–14, A).

Reinforcing Time's Cycle: Calendars and Seasons

For much of recorded history the calendar ruled over human affairs. It served as the primary instrument of social control, regulating the duration, sequence, rhythm, and tempo of life and coordinating and synchronizing the shared group activities of the culture. . . . In calendar cultures, the future takes its meaning from the past. Humanity organizes the future by continually resurrecting and honoring its past experiences. (Rifkin, 1987, p. 79)

Table 2–1   Rotten Jack: Time References

	Past	Present	Present in Relation to Past	Future
Brad	■	■		
Ming		■	■	
Kelly	■	■	■	
Nick		■	■	
Joshua	■	■		
Eugene		■	■	
Debbie	■	■	■	
Ethan		■	■	
Gwen		■	■	
TJ		■	■	
Julie		■		
Jimmy		■		
Sally		■		
Paul	■	■	■	
Claudia	■	■		
Sarah	■	■	■	
Susan	■	■		
Graham	■	■	■	■
Ashley		■	■	
Bruce		■		
Linda	■	■		

Pat McLure also reinforces our cultural view of the cyclical nature of time in the curriculum she plans for the children. In January, when they returned from their winter vacation, the class began a unit on calendars. Different corners of the room displayed examples of calendars from around the world and from past years as well as the current year, and the months of the year were listed in large letters and on a circular chart.

As the children created their own calendars, drawing pictures for each month and filling in the correct days on the month, they had other assignments that drew attention to the yearly return of certain important dates. On January 6, the children brought letters home to their parents asking for help with important dates that should be included on their calendars. Although some were the same for each child—

Figure 2–15   Claudia's Letter (Excerpt)

Dear _Mama,_____,

We have started working on calendars for the
new year - 1988. Can you please help me with important
dates?

Signed, CLAuDia

Birthdays: CLAuDia : January 30
PaPa: March 17
ROSE : July 3
Mama: July 28
~~Holidays:~~ Smoke & Matilda August 19

Holidays: Valentine's Day: February 14
St. Patrick's Day: March 17
~~Vacations:~~ Easter: April 3, 1988
LaBelle Family Day: April 17
Mother's Day: May 8
Father's Day: June 19

holidays like Halloween, for example—many were important
to individual families only.

   The birthdays were different for each family, of course,
with some children, like Claudia, including the births of her
cats, Smoky and Mathilda, for celebration. April 17 marks an
important event in her home, too—LaBelle Family Day, the
day that Claudia and her younger sister were adopted (Figure
2–15).

   The children were also expected to reflect on the four
seasons in their journals as part of this unit. Claudia experienced autumn for the first time and was most impressed by

Figure 2–16   Claudia's Fall

the falling leaves—a new phenomenon for her (Figure 2–16). During open house in October, her father recalled what a disturbing event this had been for Claudia, and how she dealt with it:

> You know, we take for granted that the leaves will fall off the trees and the grass will turn brown, and that it will all come back to life again in the spring. But Claudia has never seen this and as the trees started to become bare, she was upset. Imagine what it must have been like for her to see the whole landscape dying around her! I explained to her that the trees weren't dying, but that they were going to sleep for the winter. We had a long talk about it, and the next day when I came home from school, she was out in the yard, running her hands up and down the trunks of the trees. I didn't understand at first, but she finally made it clear to me. At night before the girls go to bed, we give them back rubs, especially rubbing their arms and legs to help them relax and get a good night's sleep. Claudia wanted the trees to get a good sleep, too.

The children all described the seasons in their own ways. In their pages on spring, for example (Figure 2–17), Kelly wrote about the hibernating animals waking up, as well as the windy but sunny weather she remembers (see Figure

Figure 2–17   Spring Stories. A: Kelly's. B: Paul's. C: Graham's.

What is spring like?
Draw and write.

All sleeping
Animals get up
Windy
a Little Bit
Sunny

a

What is spring like?
Draw and write.

IN SPRING THAR IS
MUD

b

What is spring like?
Draw and write.

SPRING IS FUN FOR
AVREAT BUT ITMENES EAT FOMR
T WADCAKS

c

2–17, A). But Paul's memories are of another aspect of the spring thaw. He wrote and drew, "In spring, there is mud" Figure 2–17, B). Graham, whose family has a huge garden, remembers that "spring is fun for everybody, but it means eating for woodchucks" (Figure 2–17, C).

Other units that Pat planned into the curriculum throughout the year also reinforced time's cycle and time's arrow. During the chick unit in the spring, for example, the children made daily observations of the hatching chickens in their classroom, sometimes speculating on the answer to the question "Which came first, the chicken or the egg?" Or the children wrote and drew careful directions for creating a snowman.

Conclusion

Time, then, is an important category in the symbols that the children work out in their writing and drawing. And they rely on both visual and verbal symbols to transfer their concepts to the page. They use their emerging literacy to learn an important social skill—an ability to "synchronize one's internal time consciousness with the cultural time of clocks" (Flaherty, 1987, p. 323). In the course of becoming socialized, children internalize the ways that their culture comprehends time. And as Flaherty points out, although children receive explicit instructions in "how to tell time," other necessary interpretations of the concept of time "tend to be neither taught nor learned in a formal fashion, but rather to be gleaned implicitly..." (p. 323).

But time isn't the only cultural concept children learn as they write and draw. They also have to learn to cope with the whole concept of representing their three-dimensional images onto the two-dimensional world of the page.

chapter three

Coping with Flatland

In his novel *Flatland: A Romance in Many Dimensions* (1884), Edwin Abbott created a two-dimensional world—a land where everything is reduced to a single plane. The people in Flatland do quite well adjusting to the constraints of their world until a stranger from Spaceland appears and tries to tell them that their houses have no walls and that he can see into their stomachs. He even goes so far as to injure his host when he reaches inside to touch the poor Flatlander's intestines. Adults often act like this bumbling Spacelander when they look at children's drawings, poking in all the wrong places and telling them what's wrong—all the while missing the power of the logic underlying the two-dimensional depictions.

As children, we all learn how to handle the constraints of the blank page. Children cope with Flatland when they create ways to show space in their messages. Gyorgy Kepes' (1969) insights into how an adult artist constructs space on a flat surface could also be applied to how children learn to use or create space:

The space which the painter tries to encompass is basically the visible order of the events he is experiencing. Painting is a form of thinking. It is, therefore, both natural and inevitable that the steps the painter takes toward formulating spatial experience are conditioned by his ideas and conceptions of the ordering of social existence.   (Kepes, 1969, p. 115)

Now take a moment to reread the quote, substituting "the child" for "the painter" and "drawing and writing" for "painting."

As children try to depict a world of depth and space on the flatness of a page, they, like the painters Kepes studied, are influenced by their abilities to perceive three-dimensional space *and* by the cultural conceptions of space that surround them.

Space Perception

Yi-Fu Tuan (1977), in his study *Space and Place: The Perspective of Experience*, argues that our concept of space is tied to our sense of our bodies:

[I]f we look for fundamental principles of spatial organization, we find them in two kinds of facts: the posture and structure of the human body, and the relations (whether close or distant) between

human beings. Man, out of his intimate experience with his body
and with other people, organizes space so that it conforms with and
caters to his biological needs and social relations. (p. 34)

Space, Tuan claims, is experienced directly as "having room
in which to move" (p. 12). Support for this claim can be
found in a linguistic analysis of the words we use to refer
to spatial relations and measurements (Thass-Thienemann,
1968). The human body has provided us with many terms of
measurement, such as foot, digit, and elbow room. Theodore
Thass-Theinemann (1968) finds that larger distances, too,
have traditionally been measured by terms implying human
action: "Such distance was the 'stone throw,' how far a man
could throw a stone or hurl a spear.... Another measure of
distance was the human voice. For instance, a garden was 'as
far from town as a man's voice will carry'" (p. 363).

In general terms, then, we organize the space we perceive
in terms of our body-sense. But what *is* this space that we
organize and perceive? What are some of the differences in
perception between child and adult or from culture to culture?

Even infants have the innate ability to recognize the
three-dimensionality of things (Yonas & Pick, 1975). But up
to about eight months, these space concepts are limited by
both physical and physiological boundaries. According to Spitz
(1965), until around that age, a child's spatial horizon is
limited by the bars of his crib. Once babies are crawling, they
can explore space—at least horizontally—and are clearly
aware of the dangers in changes of depth. Numerous studies
have shown that crawling children will refuse to crawl onto a
glass plate, even when coaxed and encouraged by parents on
the other side (Gibson, 1969).

Immediate physical perception of depth is one thing, but
what about more sophisticated elements of spatial concepts,
such as mental imaging and recognition of pictorial depth
perception? There is less agreement among theorists and psychologists in these areas.

The traditional view is that a child's spatial frame of
reference is quite restricted. Much of this is based on the
classic work of Piaget and Inhelder, *The Child's Concept of Space*
(1967). The last decade has not been kind to these theories
(see Chapter 1), but their influence remains strong in the
field. Ironically, it is through looking at children's art that
some of Piaget and Inhelder's conclusions were drawn. For

example, a child's drawing of a cowboy on his horse showed a gap between the cowboy's head and the hat. This so-called error, termed "separation," is given as evidence of a child's inability to show spatial relations among objects.

Recent research, however, points to more sophisticated spatial abilities in young children. Studies by Kosslyn (1980) and Paivio (1983) demonstrate that children as young as five years old can mentally rotate and manipulate mental images. One of Allan Paivio's (1983) simple experiments was to ask young children to picture in their minds a capital *N*. He then asked them to "tip it over on its side and tell me what it looks like." The children had no difficulty and immediately replied, "Z" (p. 15). Kosslyn's research program was more complex. He describes the basis of it in this way:

A typical respondant, if asked something like, "Do frogs have lips or stubby green tails?" would report first "looking" at the mouth of an imaged frog, then "mentally rotating" the image, and then "zooming in" on the rear to have a "close look" before answering. My research program is an effort to discover what images are, how they arise, when they are used, and what it means to "look at" and "manipulate" mental images. (p. 1)

It is important in both these studies that the stimulus be something familiar, such as letters of the alphabet. This restriction appears to hold true for older subjects as well. Familiar position is important, too; both children and adults, according to Cooper and Shepherd (1973), are much slower to rotate images when the image being matched is not in a familiar, upright position (p. 169).

Recognition of depth in pictures was once considered beyond the ability of young children, but again, researchers are being challenged to reconsider this assumption. A number of studies have demonstrated the ability of preschool children to respond to pictorial depth. Olson (1975) has shown that it is present in children at least as young as three.

That is not to say that there are not some differences between the picture perceptions of adults and children. Several studies have shown that while young children can perceive relative depth in pictures, they have a much harder time determining how far away an object is in relation to other objects on the page. "While three-year-olds perform as well as adults when asked to judge the size of actual objects placed

Figure 3–1   Horizontal Picture Space (from Hudson, 1960, p. 186)

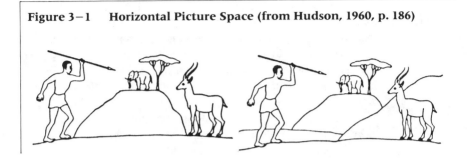

at various distances from them in an alley, when the same judgments must be made from a picture, children as old as seven are less accurate than adults" (Yonas & Pick, 1975, p. 260).

Although some theorists tie this difference to a developmental theory that picture depth perception develops independently, others believe it depends both on exposure to pictures containing depth cues and on cultural space conceptions. Hudson (1960) studied the picture depth perception of Bantu adults and children who had not been exposed to pictures before. He found that the adults who had never seen pictures were unable to perceive depth in the drawings they were shown (see Figures 3–1 and 3–2).

But it isn't that different societies perceive *picture* space differently; it is that, just like conceptions of time, space is understood in terms of the culture of which we are a part. In our culture, for example, it is common to perceive the edges

Figure 3–2   Vertical Picture Space (from Hudson, 1960, p. 187)

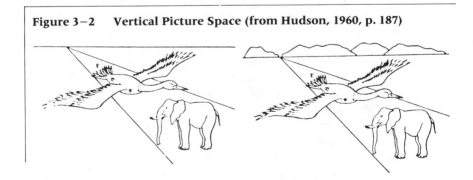

of objects. We talk of the rims of cups, the borders of gardens. Hall (1959) points out that this is a Western conception of space (p. 172). The Truk divide space much more elaborately. They treat open spaces that we perceive as having no dividing line as completely distinct, separating parts that we think of as being built in to an object. "Open spaces without obvious markers on the side of the bowl have names. Such distinctions in the dividing up of space make the settling up of land claims unbelievably complicated in these islands. Trees, for instance, are considered separate from the soil out of which they grow. One man may own the trees, the other the soil below" (p. 172).

These differences in spatial conceptions are reflected in language use as well. Benjamin Whorf (1953), in his detailed studies of American Indians' models of the universe, describes how the Hopi concepts of space are shown in their language. There are no Hopi terms "for interior three-dimensional spaces, such as words for room, chamber, hall, passage, interior, cell, crypt, cellar, attic, loft, vault. . . . In the Hopi scheme of things, a room in the strictest sense of the word is not a noun and does not act like a noun" (p. 723).

Semantic differences like this play an important role in how we perceive space. In a series of experiments on the effects of semantics on perception, Clark, Carpenter, and Just (1973) take the view that perceptual events, like linguistic events, are interpreted when they are processed. One of their studies focuses on the processing of spatial adjectives—words like shallow, deep, short, or tall. They claim that "adjectives that describe spatial relations are especially well suited for the study of the interface between linguistic and perceptual processes, for they illustrate how the same spatial relation can be conceptualized or interpreted in different ways" (p. 350). One of the most interesting of their findings is that some spatial adjectives take longer to mentally process and interpret. They conclude, for example, that "it is easier to make judgments about greater extent (longer, higher, deeper) than about lesser extent (shorter, lower, shallower)" (p. 351).

Children learn the different perceptual markers—semantic and cultural—that surround them. And as they try to transfer the three-dimensional images in their minds to the flat page before them, they rely on both verbal and visual symbols. As the children I observed tried to deal with these problems of spatial representation or, in other words, cope with Flatland, I found that they discussed the ways they could show space, wrestled with definitions of words denoting space, and worked hard to communicate their messages in this important dimension. For example, in the following exchange (transcript from field notes, November 3, 1987), Sally and Sarah are working together during writing time:

Sally: You drew right over the wheels.

Sarah: So? You colored over yours in your published book. [*Sarah keeps working on her story, writing the word "Moving" on the truck. The* g *doesn't quite fit on the side of the truck, however.*]

Sally: That *G* must be three-dimensional because it's off the truck.

Sarah: What's three-dimensional?

Sally: I'm not tellin'.

Sarah: Come on, what is it?

Sally: It's like a picture with sort of a pop-up on it without really having a pop-up.

Some children, like Sally, were able to articulate the ways that depth and space are altered on the surface of the page. But even those who didn't discuss it with metaphors to pop-up books and more sophisticated terms like "three-dimensional" solved spatial problems in the messages they wrote and drew. Some of the solutions were rather straightforward and commonly accepted conventions of our culture, such as the relationship of size depicting depth; others, like mixed perspective, were more similar to the solutions of some primitive cultures. During the children's independent writing time, I identified six distinct ways they represented spatial dimensions in their writing and drawing.

Strategies for Coping with Flatland

Relationship of Size

We are accustomed to attribute to a larger retinal projection spatial emphasis. Size, therefore, becomes the simplist statement about space. (Kepes, 1969, p. 71)

Early in the year, I began to notice instances of the children understanding and using size differences to show space. Ming was working on a story about a little man jumping on a rainbow one morning as I sat beside her. "This guy's mad,"

Figure 3–3   Ming's Rainbow Person

she explained to me. "I'll make him jumping up and mad.
He's jumping up on the rainbow. And on the next page,
you're gonna see him much closer."

"What do you mean?" I asked.

"He's gonna fill up the next page—not little and so far
away." She promptly turned the page of her writing booklet
and continued her story, just as she said (Figure 3–3).

On another day, I conferred with Kelly as she worked on
her "Sea World" story. As she worked, she narrated her
process. "Now, this is supposed to be a tuna, and these are
her fins." She thought a minute, then continued. "And I'm
going on a boat, far away, so it's little, in the corner, far away.
I'm holding little binoculars" (Figure 3–4).

These examples tend to support what Ellen Winner (1982)
terms the *constructivist theory* of perception. The constructivists
claim the following:

Although perception may seem effortless and direct. . . . this feeling
is illusory. The information available to our senses, taken by itself,
provides ambiguous and misleading information about its source;

Figure 3–4   Kelly's Sea World

perceptions are the product of constant, unconscious supplementation on the part of the perceiver. And because the information that must be supplemented is inherently ambiguous, perception is essentially a matter of guesswork.   (p. 89)

The classic example of this theory is a scene with two people, one near and one far away (see Figure 3–5). If we read this picture, or Ming's story, literally, we would perceive two people on the same plane, one person much smaller than the other. According to Helmholtz (as cited in Winner, 1982), we

Figure 3–5 **Figures Illustrating the Phenomenon of Size Constancy (from Winner, 1982, p. 89)**

are able to make these perceptual inferences because of our knowledge of the world, which is gained from experience. This also supports the view that children's understanding of some of the spatial cues is experiential rather than developmental.

Children, then, are able to make these perceptual inferences when they are drawing and when they are reading. As Sally read and shared *Caps for Sale*, she noted that the peddler must be very far away. Later in the year, I sat in on a book-sharing conference among three children, Jimmy, Ashley, and Nick. When Jimmy shared *Dan, the Flying Man*, he looked at the receding figures in an endless parade and noted, "Look, these guys are smaller. They're so far away, you can't even see their eyes." These children are making

Figure 3-6   Graham's Nature Museum Measure

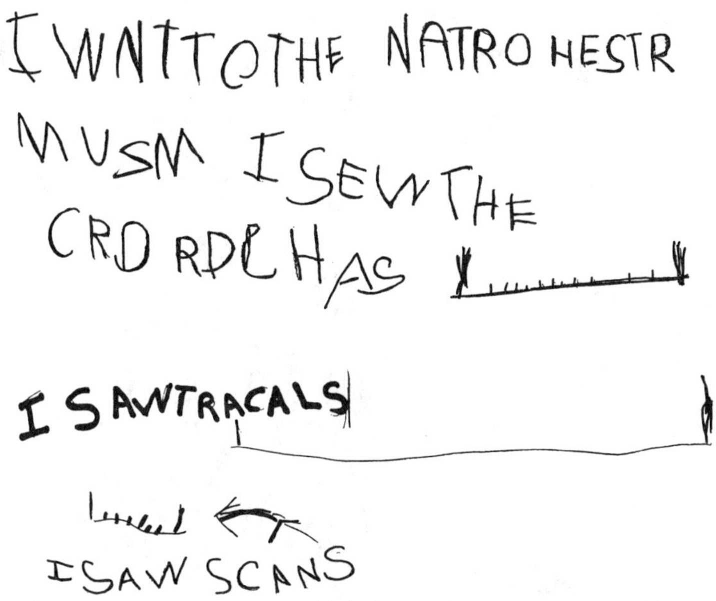

I WNTTOTHE NATRO HESTR
MUSM I SEW THE
CRD RDLH AS
I SAWTRACALS
I SAW SCANS

inferences daily in their reading of the *whole* text, both verbally and visually. They become familiar with the conventions they see in books, and this, to some extent, may influence the way they express notions of depth and space in their stories.

But they are not solely imitators; they also *invent* ways to show size differences. Consider Graham's writing and drawing of his trip to a science museum (Figure 3-6). He was fascinated by the different creatures that he saw in the nature section of the museum and wanted to show the difference in their sizes. "I went to the Nature Museum," he began. In an effort to show the relative sizes of the insects he saw, he then drew a ruler measure next to the words of each. "I saw cockroaches" is written next to a marked line of approximately three inches. Similar lines of varying length follow the texts of "I saw tarantulas" and "I saw scorpions." And because the scorpions are smaller, there is even a little arrow drawn to tie the words and measure together.

Figure 3—7   Nick's Presents

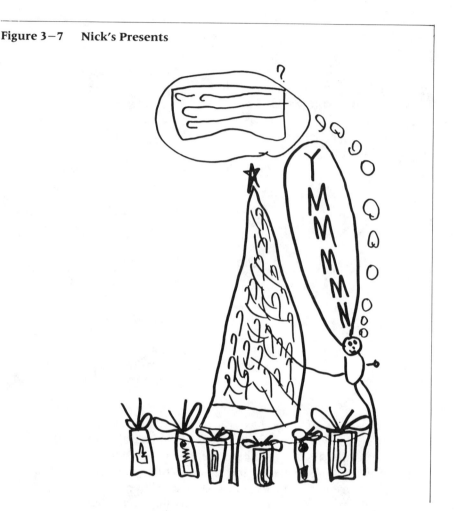

Transparency

Another way that children represent space is to create drawings that allow the viewer to see through an object to something behind or inside it. Nick shared such an example one morning a few days before Christmas vacation. He had drawn his Christmas tree with all the presents under it. Even though they were wrapped, *we* could easily see inside. However, his brother Mark, who is in the picture, could not (Figure 3—7).

"There's something inside all the presents, see?" Nick explained. "That's a fish, a Jack-in-the-box, candy canes, a new stockin', a rattle for Will. And that guy is my brother Mark. He loves candy canes. He's thinkin' he's gonna ask Mom if he can have the biggest candy cane on the tree."

Other children solve the problem of overlapping figures occupying the same space by creating the same kind of transparency that Nick did. Linda, for example, recorded in her choice book what she had worked on during Free Choice Time in the afternoon: "Me and Ashley used the computer," she wrote (Figure 3–8). In her picture, she wanted to show what it looked like to an observer watching her and Ashley working—a view of their backs as they faced the computer screen with the Logo turtle on it. She wanted to show *how* they were creating the Logo drawing using the keyboard, but their backs blocked this view. She solved the problem by making the figures transparent, thereby giving the observer a simultaneous image of different spatial locations.

These kinds of drawings have been termed *X-ray* drawings by some researchers (Gardner, 1982; Winner, 1982; and Freeman, 1980). These theorists conclude that children "are simply unable to draw in a more realistic way" (Winner, 1982, p. 158). Although Winner concedes that there are "surface parallels" between the child's use of space and some adult artists, she concludes that they may have "no alternative but to make X-ray drawings. And they may not intend the strong visual effect they create" (p. 160).

I disagree with these conclusions and with the notion that these *are* X-ray drawings. These researchers did not talk to the children whose drawings they examined, nor did they know the children's other work. In the case of Nick and Linda, these children *do* have alternatives to showing space, but chose in these instances to use transparency to solve the particular visual problem at hand. In reviewing Nick's writing folder from September to January, I found this was the only time he chose to use this kind of transparency, and he used it because he specifically wanted to show that *we* knew what was in those presents but that his brother Mark didn't. In all Nick's stories about the zoo and the animals he saw eating there, he did no drawings denoting the food inside their stomachs, a hallmark of Freeman's (1980) "X-ray drawing phase."

Figure 3–8   **Linda's Choice Book**

I prefer to use the term *transparency* for this solution to showing space on the page because this is a technique artists purposefully use. Although psychologists like Winner would term the similarities to Chagall's "Pregnant Woman"—where the artist draws the baby inside the transparent uterus of its mother—only surface, I believe that the children, like the artist, are consciously solving the problems of space.

Figure 3–9 **Sally's Trip**

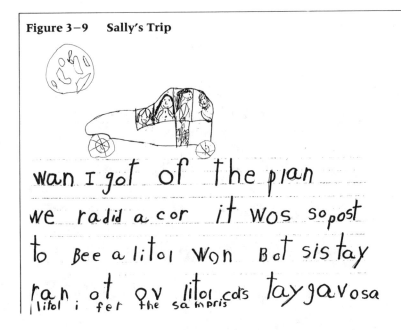

wan I got of the plan
we radid a cor it wos sopost
to Bee a litol Won Bot sis tay
ran ot ov litol cots tayjavosa
litol i fer the sa mpris

Sally's story about her trip to visit her grandparents provides more evidence of how children consciously solve spatial problems (Figure 3–9). She wrote about the car they rented ("since they ran out of little cars"), and she wanted her readers to know what it was like inside the car as well as outside. First she drew the car with all its occupants in the right order, her bearded dad in front driving, and she and her sister in the back seat looking out at the craters in the moon. But inside the car, she told me, "It was a mess! We had Pepsi on the floor, crayons, books, blocks." In the rectangle drawn under her mom, we can see all the items she mentioned—we get a view of both the inside and outside. At this point, I thought she was done with this page and made a copy during recess.

I was premature in my judgment, however, as I believe other researchers may have been in the past. The next day, when Sally returned to her writing, she had come up with a modification of how she wanted to show the inside and outside of her car. She cut out and taped a door over the car's side, which opens and closes to reveal—and to hide—the mess on the floor inside (Figure 3–10).

Figure 3–10   Sally's Trip (Modified)

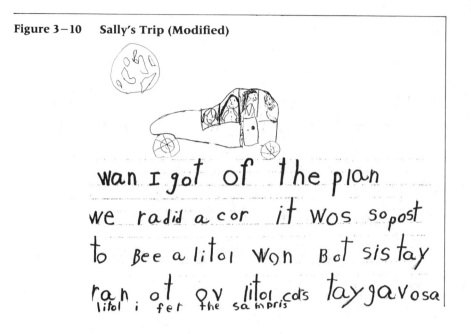

wan I got of the plan
we radid a cor it wos sopost
to Bee a litol Won Bot sistay
ran ot ov litol cats taygavosa
litol i fer the sampris

Overlapping Figures

Another way to create a sense of depth on the page is to have
one form obstruct our view of part of another form. Medieval
artists often overlapped figures as a way of bringing some
figures nearer to the viewer (Figure 3–11). I found many
children in the class overlapping objects in this way, an ability
overlooked by the researchers who find only examples of X-
ray drawings at this stage.

Ming used this overlapping technique often. Early in the
year, when she wrote about her cat running away from her
dog, only half of the dog's body is drawn so we can easily
perceive that her dog is behind the house (Figure 3–12).

Later in the year, she used the same technique but in a
more sophisticated manner (Figure 3–13). This time, she
drew her body parallel to the picture plane but overlapped
one of her arms so that only the tip of her elbow showed—
clearly on a plane further back from the viewer. "I'm going to
the contest," she wrote, then explained, "I've got my fingers
crossed behind my back, hoping and hoping I'll win the prize
for my pumpkin."

Figure 3–11 Overlapping Figures: *Madonna Surrounded by Saints* from the Aldobrini Triptych (ca. 1336) by a Follower of Bernado Daddi (Collection of the Portland Art Museum, Oregon, Gift of the Samuel H. Kress Foundation)

Figure 3–12   Ming's Dog

MY CAT IS TOW
TO LIKY A DOY

On another day, Kelly wrote about the things you can do at recess and created three planes of depth in her drawing of the merry-go-round (Figure 3–14). Nearest to us is Kelly as she approaches the equipment, one plane back is a child standing on top of it, while in the furthest plane from us a child is behind the equipment, sitting on the other side of it, the wood overlapping so our view of her legs is obstructed. Kelly explained that this child "is sitting on it the right way, so it's safe, not standing on it the wrong way."

Figure 3–13   The Pumpkin Contest

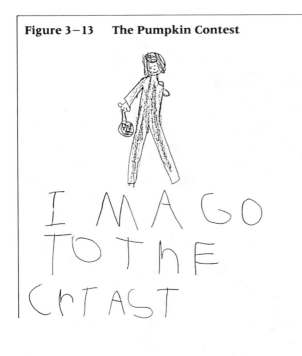

I M A GO
TO T h E
C h T AST

Figure 3–14   Kelly's Merry-Go-Round

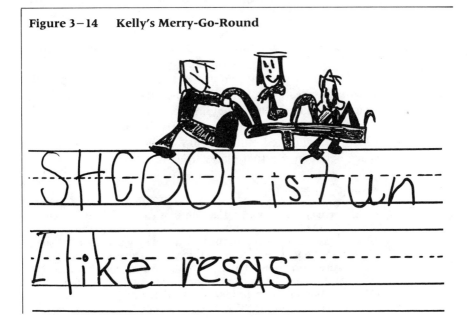

SHCOOL is Fun

I like resas

Figure 3–15   Paul's Cat

This is also something children notice in the books they read. In *Dan the Flying Man*, Jimmy commented on how he could tell the man was bending over the mountain top in the picture, his head and shoulders covering the rest of his body as he leaned over. In his reading journal, Paul drew a picture of a cat based on the photograph of a cat in his book. The tail of the cat emerged from behind its head, emphasizing the space between the two planes (Figure 3–15).

Mixed Perspective

In primitive art, [two things] have been attempted: the perspective as well as showing the essential parts in combinations. Since the essential parts are symbols of the object, we may call this method the symbolic one. I repeat that in the symbolic method those features are represented that are considered as permanent and essential, and that there is no attempt on the part of the draftsman to confine himself to a reproduction of what he actually sees at a given moment.   (Boas, 1955, p. 91)

Figure 3–16   Claudia's House

Like the early artists Boas (1955) studied, children seem to take the realistic view that they will do whatever is necessary for their particular visual purpose. They appear to accept that things can be presented at a size and angle that best fits the situation without worrying whether this visual correctness is true to nature.

One morning in September, I observed two children trying to work out perspective. Through gesture and some English, Claudia was explaining to me about her two cats, who don't like each other. Joshua, sitting at a nearby desk, joined our conversation, mentioning that he has two cats, too. He had already drawn a house with windows, and now he decided to add his two cats to the drawing. Claudia, on the other hand, decided she, like Joshua, would draw her house.

As she worked on her house, she explained it to me (Figure 3–16). The windows were very important to her because they defined her room. She explained that she had even drawn the shades "so you can pull down." And beside the front view of her house, she included the windows of her room that the viewer wouldn't see from the front. We are treated to a simultaneous view of all parameters—all four windows—that define her bedroom.

Later, when I went back to Joshua, I realized that independently, he had used the same technique of multiple perspective to solve space problems in his story (Figure 3–17). Here, beside the front view of his house, the cats are shown from a different perspective—all four legs and their entire faces simultaneously, as if from the top. As Joshua struggled to write "C" for cat and "H" for house, Kelly poked her head over to ask, "Is that a side view?"

Figure 3–17   Joshua's House

"No," Joshua answered shortly, more involved in his writing now. "I have to erase this 'C'—it's too pointy." Joshua's intent was apparently not to present a side view but to show more of the dimensions.

Side views and top views are very important to Kelly in her own writing and drawing, too. She included both on one page in her dog sled story (Figure 3–18). She explained to me, "Over here's a side view of the water hole, and over here's a top view. I wanted to make it look like it would swing and make waves right off the paper."

Figure 3–18   Kelly's Water Hole

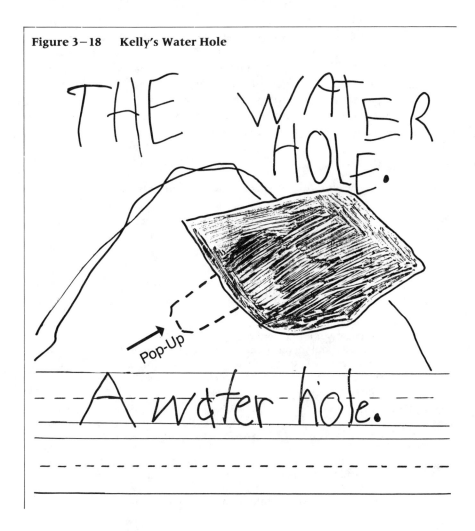

When Eugene created his calendar in January, he included all kinds of animals that interest him: dinosaurs, reptiles, and, for the month of March, a drawing of an amphibian (Figure 3−19). From the top view, the scales on the back of its neck are clearly visible. At the same time, viewers are able to see all four webbed feet, almost as if we are looking up from underneath the creature's belly.

When Linda drew her living room at Christmastime, she wanted her audience to see it just as it really was, with all the details available in a three-dimensional world (Figure 3−20). She wanted us to see both the front view of the television set and the top view of the dials and knobs on the VCR on top of it. Her Christmas tree is parallel to the picture plane, but the chair recedes into the corner. The angle of the lights on the ceiling is as if the viewer were underneath looking straight up, but the edges of the lumber in the floor are from a perspective looking straight down. It is as if we are in the midst of the room, looking at all of its angles, yet viewing it from an outside picture window, simultaneously.

Bird's-Eye View

Besides looking at several views simultaneously, children also draw from a perspective they rarely see themselves—from the top looking down. Yet they seem able to understand, and to render, how things look from a bird's-eye view.

In an early study of children's cognitive abilities, Susan Isaacs (1930) gives this example of very young children exploring spatial relations as they created a model of a garden as it looked to a man in an "aeroplane."

Some of the children climbed "as high up the ladder as we can get, to see how it looks from the plane." One boy of four-and-a-half realized spontaneously that from the plane, only the tops of their own heads would be seen, and he dotted a number of small, flat ovals over the paths of the model, "That's the children running about." (p. 37)

Tuan (1977) also marvels at children's ability to understand aerial perspective.

Children are small people in a world of giants and gigantic things not made to their scale. Yet children five or six years old show remarkable understanding of how landscapes look from above. They can read black-and-white aerial photographs with unexpected

Figure 3–19   Eugene's Amphibian

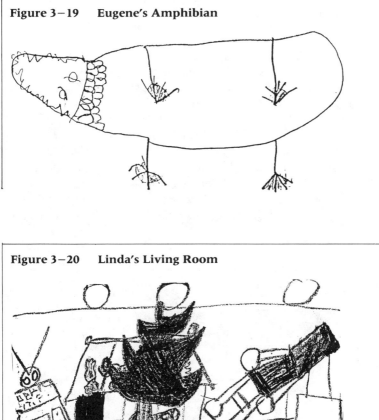

Figure 3–20   Linda's Living Room

accuracy and confidence. They can pick out the houses, roads, and
trees on aerial photographs even though these features appear
greatly reduced in scale and are viewed from an angle and position
unknown to them in actual experience.   (p. 27)

    I noticed the children drawing from this perspective on
the first day of school. Claudia's first piece of writing, for
example, shows an aerial view of the desks in the classroom
(Figure 3–21).

    But some of the other examples show a more complicated
view of the scene from above. Nick used an aerial perspective
in his "Secret Plan for Snack Recess" (Figure 3–22). He
explained it this way: "This is our plan for snack recess. We
jump out of the cement block, get on the merry-go-round, sit
on it for two minutes, then get off, go to the one-headed
slide...."

Figure 3–21   Claudia's Classroom

Figure 3–22   Nick's Secret Plan for Snack Recess

"Wait a minute," I interrupted. "What's a one-headed slide?"

"It has only one beam." Nick continued, "Go down that once, then go down to the pole. Then go behind the pole. Go down it. Then, we attack Aja. We bring her back to the base." For creating a secret and rather complicated plan like this, an aerial view that takes in the whole playground scene was clearly helpful.

Sometimes the children's top-down views were more abstract, showing a sophisticated understanding of this concept. One morning, I overheard Megan and Graham discussing perspective and Christopher Columbus as they colored in pictures about the Pledge of Allegiance after a class discussion on American symbols.

Megan: But how did he find out the world is round?
[*Graham draws a diagram on his paper—Figure 3–23.*]
Graham: People thought it was a big rectangle, like a pencil with monsters at each end.
[*Next, Graham draws a diagram of the world.*]
Graham: See? Then he sailed around the earth. Here's England. Here's his ship. He's already gone this far on this map here. He spots England again, and he knows the earth is round. And here's another map—the boat's in England, he sees England, then he lands in England.
[*Megan draws a line on her book.*]
Megan: Not a rectangle.
Graham: You did yours different. I'm doing it from overhead.
(Transcript from field notes, September 16, 1987)

Combination of Words and Pictures

There were also examples in the writing of almost all the children in the class, where the words and pictures worked together to define space. For example, in Paul's story about a man in space, he wanted to show how the position of the spaceman affected him. He drew and cut out a figure first, carefully making the hair stand up to show what "it's like with no gravity." But words were definitely needed to show what happened to the man: "The man went upside down" (Figure 3–24).

Figure 3–23   Graham's Diagram

Figure 3-24 Paul's Spaceman

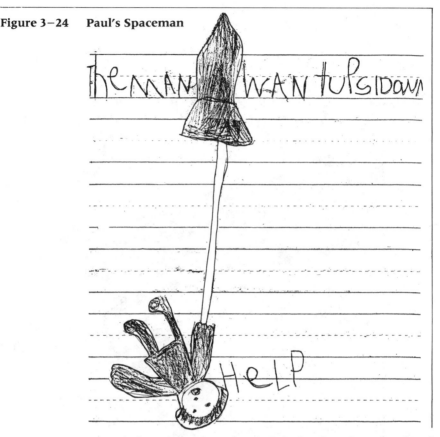

In Linda's story about her hand, she first drew her hand with her new bracelet on it, but was dissatisfied with the results (Figure 3–25, A). She needed the preposition "on" to show where the bracelet was: "I have my bracelet on my hand" (Figure 3–25, B).

Prepositions were, in fact, by far the most frequently used linguistic spatial markers in the children's writing, the most prevalent being *in* and *on*. Others often used by the children were *over*, *at*, *into*, and *behind*. Adjectives common in their speaking vocabularies—words like *tall* or *deep*—were virtually absent from their writing. There were a few children like Kelly, who would occasionally use specific distance terms, as in her volcano story, when she swam "ten miles away." But classwide, prepositions accounted for more than 90 percent of the words children used to express space in their writing.

Figure 3–25   Linda's Bracelet Story

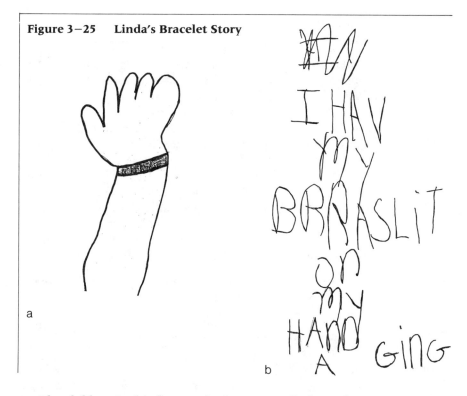

a

b

The children in this first-grade classroom relied mainly on six strategies for coping with Flatland when they transferred their three-dimensional images to the page:

- Relationship of size.
- Transparency.
- Overlapping figures.
- Mixed perspective.
- Bird's-eye view.
- Combination of words and pictures.

Besides these six categories, I found other ways that some children chose to extend the concept of space on the page. Pop-ups, for example (which are discussed in more detail in Chapter 4), were sometimes used to create a third dimension; and Kelly occasionally used the front and back of her paper to extend some of her characters off the page. These uses, however, were not used widely enough to create a category for this particular group of children.

Space in Rotten Jack

In their Rotten Jack journals, the children also needed to represent three-dimensional space, but I found that this situation caused the children to rely more heavily on some categories than on others. All the children but one, Bruce, used words and pictures together to create space. In fact, all these children used prepositions specifically, words like *around, inside, in, on, under,* and *outside.* The next largest category was the bird's-eye view. Thirteen of the twenty-two children used this technique. This view was helpful to show what the pumpkin looked like after it had fallen from the shelf. The technique of overlapping was used only once, and relationship of size not at all (see Table 3−1). The results of this survey show, I believe, that the children were flexible in their choice

Table 3−1   Rotten Jack: Spatial Symbols

	Transparency	Overlapping	Mixed Perspective	Bird's-eye	Words & Pictures
Brad					■
Ming	■	■		■	■
Kelly			■	■	■
Nick					■
Joshua				■	■
Eugene				■	■
Debbie			■		■
Ethan					■
Gwen				■	■
TJ					■
Julie				■	■
Jimmy					■
Sally					■
Paul				■	■
Claudia			■	■	■
Sarah			■		■
Megan			■	■	■
Susan				■	■
Graham	■		■		■
Ashley			■	■	■
Bruce				■	
Linda				■	■

of ways to represent space, using the techniques that best fit the demands of the situation.

The drawings that the children did for their Rotten Jack journals illustrate how they used different techniques to achieve different spatial effects. Ming drew herself touching Rotten Jack on the nose when she wrote, "At Jack's nose, it is soft" (Figure 3–26, A). On this page, she wanted to show that she was on the plane in front of the pumpkin, and the overlapping technique helped her solve this space problem best. Graham, on the other hand, wanted to show himself reaching inside and under Jack's nose for his observation "Jack is mushy under his nose," so the conscious use of transparency made sense (Figure 3–26, B). When Rotten Jack fell to the floor, many children, like Paul, used the bird's-eye view to show how all the pieces looked on the floor (Figure 3–26, C). Others, like Debbie, preferred to use mixed perspective to show the pumpkin and shelf from the side, and then an overhead view to show those pieces when "Rotten Jack fell down off the shelf" (Figure 3–26, D). Twenty-one out of twenty-two children found there was no better alternative than a combination of words and pictures to express spatial details, like Ashley's "He has some black spots on the outside" (Figure 3–26, E).

Figure 3–26   Rotten Jack Journals. A: Ming—Overlapping. B: Graham—Transparency. C: Paul—Bird's-Eye View. D: Debbie—Mixed Perspective. E: Ashley—Words and Pictures.

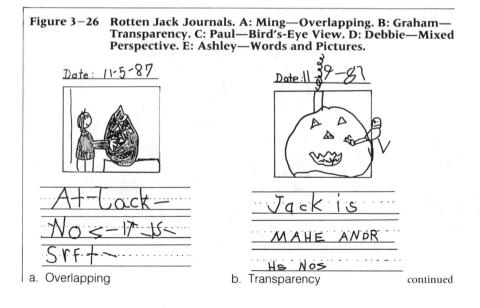

a. Overlapping   b. Transparency   continued

Figure 3–26   Continued

Date: 11-9-87

s| rotten JACK
KLAPST

c. Bird's-Eye View

Date: 11-8-87

rotten Jock
fAl Down
off the
Shelve

d. Mixed Perspective

Date: 11-3-87

he has
some blak
spots on the
outside

e. Words and Pictures

Conclusion

Of all the aspects of children's pictorial representation, by far the most research and conjecture has been on their use of space. Unfortunately, most experimenters are not looking at the nature of the task, the child's intentions to communicate, or the logic they use when coping with the demands of transferring their three-dimensional images to a single plane.

The six-year-old children I observed made rational, deliberate decisions when representing space. They used, for example, our cultural understanding of the relationship of size to show how near and how far away people are. They represented what's inside an object by deliberately drawing it as transparent. And they relied on words—especially spatial markers like prepositions—to complement the drawings on their pages.

They solved other problems as well. The images and events that the children wanted to communicate were not static images, frozen in space and time; they often danced, leaped, and whirled. When young children transfer images onto paper, they also find solutions to the problem of representing movement, as the next chapter shows.

chapter four

Pieces of the Action: Children's Symbols for Movement

Eugene looks up from his writing folder to explain to Kelly, sitting next to him, "I'm drawin' the biggest plant in the world. I can't pronounce it, but it's some kind of huge cactus."

Kelly continues intently with her work as she responds. "I'm makin' something," then sounds out carefully, "I am on the bus." She looks at her work critically, then starts making sweeping circular lines with her pencil. Eugene peers at her paper, interested. "This isn't the bus," she tells him. "I'm scribblin' for...to make the bus look like it's moving."

Eugene nods and points to his paper. "You wanta see somethin'? That's an elf hole."

But Kelly doesn't look up—instead, she keeps explaining her process. "The bus is bouncing out of its wheels." She smiles and draws vertical action lines. "It's jumpin', really—even more—like this."

As children attempt to communicate their action-filled stories, memories, and mental images onto the surface of a page, they are faced with the same problem many artists face. "The principal problem to be explained," writes John L. Ward (1979), "is how movement can be represented when a painter is only able to give us a piece—or, at best, pieces—of the action. How can the movement of a figure, which happens over time, be shown in the timeless medium of a picture?" (p. 246).

Surprisingly, the many theorists and psychologists who study the fields of child development and symbolic representation in general have paid little attention to the depiction of motion in children's drawing and writing. This may be because traditional developmentalists adhere to the Piagetian view that children's internal imagery does not preserve the "qualities of motion" (See Piaget & Inhelder, 1971; and Dean, 1976). These conclusions are based on research that does not measure the *child's* intentions to communicate motion. Piaget and Inhelder, for example, asked children to draw a falling stick. The children complied, but did not represent the continuity or the proper trajectory of the falling stick. In the experimenters' view, the children failed to represent motion—according to their preconceived ideas of the way to represent the movement of a falling stick. There are two obvious shortcomings to this research. The first deals with intentionality. The children drew falling sticks because they were asked by adults to do so; they did not necessarily have an intent or

desire to communicate that information. Secondly, the experimenters had preconceived notions of the correct way to depict motion. Others who are in the children's culture may have understood the children's solutions.

The lack of research in the study of motion carries over into the world of adults as well. Gibson (1969) and Goodman (1968), for example, offer the most in-depth recent theories of picture representation, but they do not include any discussion of the problem of showing movement. For those researchers who *do* discuss it, it becomes a debate between innate perception abilities and cultural influences.

Rudolf Arnheim (1974) takes the extreme position that motion in pictures is understood purely perceptually. It is, he contends, a visual interpretation of reality—the "dynamic composition" must be balanced and this in turn activates the brain processes to interpret motion (p. 416).

Ernst Gombrich (1961), on the other hand, emphasizes that picture representations are culture specific. He believes that picture movement must be supplied by the viewer's imagination; just like reading print, reading pictures depends on reconstructing what has happened and anticipating what will happen. "Two qualities will therefore enhance the effectiveness of depicted movement: clarity of meaning (the viewer must be able to understand what is happening in order to understand how it has developed and will develop over time) and unclarity or incompleteness of form, which will arouse in the viewer the memories and anticipations of movement" (p. 306).

Gombrich's view is appealing to me because it ties in with my theoretical framework for reading processes. Just as viewers interpret pictures based on their background experiences and their cultural biases, so do readers have personal associations to words—and to the referents to those words in a literary text (Rosenblatt, 1978). Norman Holland's (1968) psychoanalytic approach to literary response goes even further, suggesting that the way we interpret texts is the way we interpret our worlds—in terms of our own identity.

This identity is necessarily part of the society in which we are raised. Culture, at least partially, influences the way we interpret motion in pictures. Certain conventions, such as the cartoon-type action lines and multiple drawings to represent motion, appear to be Western conventions, understood by children in our society as young as three years old but not by people in other cultures. In a study among Bantu and white schoolchildren in South Africa, Duncan, Gourlay, and Hudson (1973) found that only 3 percent of rural Zulus thought that the pictures in Figure 4–1, A, represented motion, while 86 percent of the Western subjects interpreted the child's head to be moving. And in response to the picture in Figure 4–1, B, only 1 percent of the rural Zulus and 3 percent of the rural Tsongas thought the dog was moving, yet 75 percent of the European subjects "knew" the dog was running and wagging its tail. Other studies, of the Bantu and the Songe of Papua, lend support to the notion that perception of motion in pictures is culturally influenced. (See also Winter, 1963; and Kennedy & Ross, 1975.)

As members of Western society, the children in Pat McLure's class understood and used both these conventions to show motion in their pictures. They also used and invented much more: in analyzing the symbols they used in their drawing and writing, I identified seven categories that describe how they represented their "pieces of the action."

Figure 4–1   Action Lines—Boy and Dog (from Duncan, Gourlay, and Hudson, 1973, p. 26)

a   b

Children's Symbols for Movement

Multiple Images

One morning, Graham was intent on communicating a "terrifying" experience during writing time. He explained to me his drawing of falling off a swing (Figure 4−2). "That's the swing at different times," he told me, pointing to the two swings on the page. "It was going up and it had to go down." He rolled his eyes and gave an exaggerated shudder. "I did a backwards somersault right off the swing! Boy, did that give me a headache! See? I'm goin' back. I'm goin' up, I fall back, I roll over, and that is it."

One way to represent movement on a page is to show an object or a person in successive moments over time, as Graham did. These multiple images tend to indicate movement that occurs in a brief amount of time. I found that the children often used this technique to show movement, especially that of the human body. Nick found it helpful in his epic circus chronicle, "I Went to the Circus" (Figure 4−3). As he explained it to the class during whole-class sharing time, "This guy was walking on this tightrope, walking. . . . And he's there, and he walked across, and then he fell. 'Boom! Oh, no!'"

Figure 4−2   Graham's Swing Accident

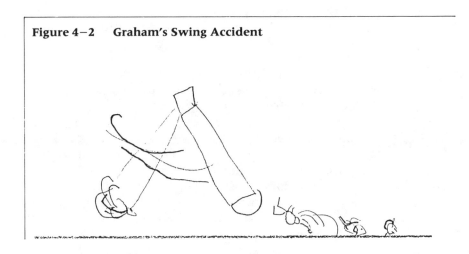

Figure 4–3   **Nick's Chronicle "I Went to the Circus"**

The audience appreciated this depiction, directing many of their comments and questions to this particular page. It was Ethan's favorite part: "I like the part where you have him walk the tightrope, and he says, 'Oh, no!'" This gave Nick a chance to re-explain his solution. Turning to the page again, he chuckled, "Yeah...that? See, he fell down, and he's there, and...."

"Is that tightroper part true?" Ming asked, suddenly concerned about the thought of the performer actually falling to the ground.

"No, some of the parts are true, and some aren't."

Art theorist Gyorgy Kepes (1969) states that this use of multiple images, especially for body parts, was one of the earliest solutions painters attempted to suggest movement on a stationary surface. Like children, early men and women knew that changes serve to suggest movement. "The prehistoric artist knew his animals, knew, for example, how many legs they had. But when he saw an animal in really speedy movement, he could not escape seeing the visual modification of the known spatial characteristics" (p. 173). In my pilot study, I found many instances of children repeating images to show the movement of balls and other objects. In the present study, however, this didn't appear. During the first study, I think the repetition of images was partly a social phenomenon. The children in the previous class saw it used and found it useful for their purposes, so it spread, much like the pop-up convention discussed later in this chapter.

Movement "As It Happens"

In our Western culture, children begin to make marks, often called scribbles, at a very young age. Various researchers who have studied preschool children note the importance of motor activity over content, or even color, on the page (Gibson, 1966). But it is more than the actual arm movement across the page that is important to these young children. In an interesting experiment, Gibson and Yonas (1968) replaced children's markers with ones that didn't leave any traces. Even children below two years of age soon lost interest in the scribbling *if* it left no marks. Gibson and Yonas conclude that not only are children interested in the physical action of scribbling, they are also very interested in the traces—that record of their motor activity that they have left on the page.

This carries over into the way school-age children show movement as well. The actual activity they are immersed in—scribbling or acting out an event on the page—is partly action and play in the midst of their composing. But it also serves the important purpose of *symbolizing* that action on the page itself. Kelly, for example, was intrigued with a story about an oil tank exploding that she saw on television. My first impression of her from across the room was that she was "just fooling around and scribbling this morning," but I was wrong.

"Look at this gas exploding!" Kelly demanded, as she pushed her writing booklet toward me (see Figure 4—4). Her scribbles were a way for her to act out the motion she was trying to understand from the explosion she saw on the news, but when she explained it to me, it had become an actual symbol of that action.

The children seemed to depict movement on the page "as it happened" when they were working out something new, like Kelly's gas explosion. Claudia had many new concepts and experiences to understand in our different climate and culture. In the early fall, she showed me a sheet of paper with

Figure 4–4   Kelly's Explosion

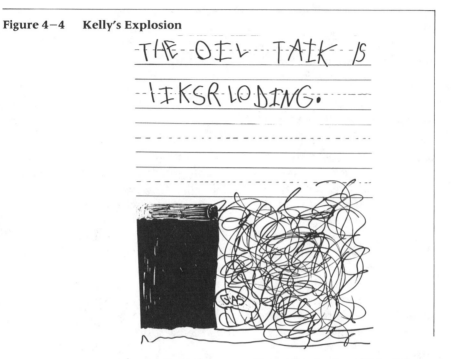

no words on it, only some lines she had scribbled down
(Figure 4–5). This was different from the usual writing she
was attempting at this time, copying symbols and words from
her surroundings into her writing booklet.

She looked expectantly at me as she showed me the page,
so I asked her to tell me about it. "Wind. Wind. Brrrr," she
clutched her arms and demonstrated that the wind she was
writing about was cold, a real aberration from the warm
climate she had known in Portugal.

"Wind? Write?" she asked

"Wind," I repeated slowly. "/w/, /w/...."

Claudia looked up at the picture alphabet on the wall.

"It's /w/, double-u, like the whale, see?"

Claudia shrugged impatiently, "No write," then made her
"eh" sound (accompanied by an upturned hand), and looked
again at the way she had written the cold wind on the paper.
She was content to work it out her own way for now—that
tricky double-u sound would have to wait.

Debbie's writing one morning began as a page of brilliant
balloons (Figure 4–6). As I watched, she put her crayons and
markers away and started to scribble over the page with her

Figure 4–5   Claudia's Lines—"Wind"

Figure 4–6   Debbie's Balloons

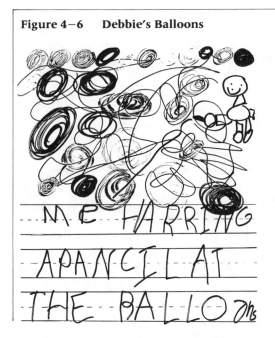

pencil, a smile touching her lips as her arm completed up-and-down and circular motions across the page. "This is me, poppin' balloons," she told me.

"Can you tell me about the pencil marks?" I asked.

"It's a path where I can pop all the balloons with one pencil! In the picture, I'm throwing pencils at the balloons." She then flipped back the pages and read me her whole book, "a book about things." Her last page ended with the words "Me, throwing a pencil at the balloons." She was well pleased with the motion she depicted, even choosing to share this writing with the class several days later, pointing out again the path the pencil took as it scurried across the page and finally flew through the air in her mental image.

The Frozen Moment

Another way to represent motion on a picture surface is to choose one moment in the process of movement and freeze it. Goodnow (1978) discusses children's ability to indicate movement in this way with the term "single viewpoint, single moment." He points out that children rely on a sideways representation of a figure or object to show that single moment.

Kelly's reading journal about Paul Bunyan exemplifies just such a frozen moment (Figure 4–7). "Paul Bunyan fights the monster plants," reads her text. She relies on a frozen side view of Paul swinging an axe at the plant, the weapon frozen above his head. Kelly chose her moment well; her audience knows that the axe cannot remain in this position for long, so it's interpreted as an axe swinging in the air. The side view is helpful to mark the moment clearly, and the bent arm is exaggerated, a technique Arnheim (1974) found employed by adult artists.

But it's not just this single viewpoint that children employ; the choice of a particular moment in the action is also key. When moments are chosen well, we, as viewers, use the whole context of the situation to interpret the movement of the physical world we know. When Megan chose to draw her witch's frog flying through the air, she succeeded in representing this movement because the viewer knows that the frog can't remain in flight long and so is actually moving through the air (Figure 4–8).

Figure 4–7   Kelly's Paul Bunyan

Figure 4–8   Megan's Frog

Figure 4–9   **Satyr Pursuing a Maenad (Column Krater, Attic Red-
                Figured, ca. 480 B.C., Collection of the Portland Art Museum,
                Oregon; the Sally Lewis Collection of Classical Antiquities)**

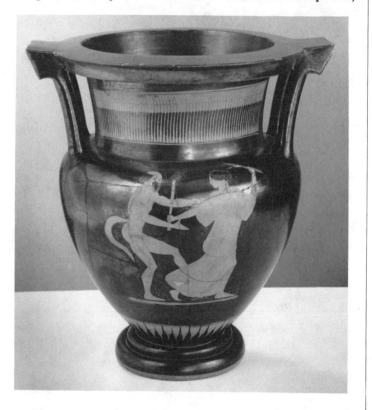

A frozen body posture can also be particularly effective in
showing movement. In Figure 4–9, the Greek figures show
by their poses that they are in the midst of a chase. Seven-
year-old Graham used this same technique when he wanted
to show how dizzy he got at the Omni theatre. "I'm a little
dizzy," he explained. "Those are the lights, that's the camera
operator." Then he pointed to the representation of himself,
toes pointed in, arms extended, stars in his eyes, as he staggers
through the theatre in his dizzy state (Figure 4–10). "I'm
walking like this 'cause I'm so dizzy," he explained.

Figure 4–10   Graham at the Omni Theatre

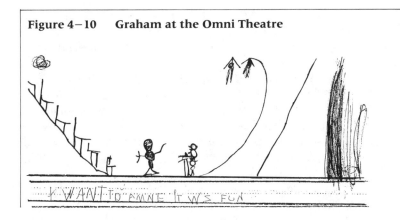

Metaphor

Sometimes, movement is suggested through a kind of pictorial metaphor (Friedman & Stevenson, 1980). "For example, the artist may add arms and legs to an object that is limbless in reality" (p. 229). Friedman and Stevenson consider this to be a more advanced form of movement representation, "better understood by older and more acculturated subjects" (p. 232). They base their conclusions on a number of experiments where children and adults of various ages and cultural groups were shown picture metaphors for movement. According to the researchers, younger children did not correctly interpret their picture metaphors, nor did members of nonpictorial cultures.

I interpret these results differently. It seems clear from the adult responses from nonpictorial cultures that the inability to recognize the movement metaphors was dependent on exposure and experience rather than developmental ability. The particular picture metaphors that were used present another problem. They were cartoonlike representations of a rather bizarre nature, such as an alarm clock kicking a kite or a fork carrying a chair.

I am indebted to Friedman and Stevenson for the term *picture metaphor*, for I found examples of its use among the first graders I studied. But unlike these researchers, I found a sophisticated use of picture metaphors that the children were able to create as well as interpret when they wanted to communicate movement in their stories.

Graham was hard at work one day writing about his trip to New York City. "We wondered when we would get to New York City," the text reads, and the picture metaphorically explains the situation (Figure 4–11).

"That's my family in our car right there," he pointed to the vehicle in the middle of the page. "See all those marks around the wheels? They're like on tanks. You know, they show the tires are, like, diggin' in slow."

I must have looked confused because he turned to Ethan for help in his explanation. "Ethan, you know those things on tanks. What are they called?"

"Oh, I know what you mean, like on tanks? Aren't they caterpillar wheels or something like that?"

"Yeah, that's what I mean. You know? Our car was goin' along real slow, like a tank would go."

"Oh, I see what you mean," I responded. "Tell me about the rest."

"Well, see, that's my dad driving. He's going 'Mmm,' singing away, 'cause he doesn't care that we're going slow.

Figure 4–11   Graham's Trip to New York City

But that car behind us..." he pointed to the car behind them, drawn with a huge angry mouth full of teeth on its hood. "That's a New York car! He's saying, 'Hey, You!!! Beep.'"

Graham's pictorial metaphor immediately struck home for me, a timid New Hampshire driver who has experienced the *Jaws*-like aggression of impatient New York drivers!

Kelly also relied on picture metaphors to get across pieces of the action. Her entire sled dog story is an example of an attempt to make movement clear within the limits of her medium, incorporating the elements of time and space to help her (Figure 4–12). Her title page uses time: she draws just part of the dog to show he's moving (Figure 4–12, A). "This picture just has part of the dog, 'cause he's gone ahead," she explained to me.

Later in the story, she also struggled with finding the right technique to represent the motion of the water in all its dimensions. "Over here's the side view of the water hole [Figure 4–12, B], and over here's a top view [Figure 4–12, C]." Then, she created a pop-up version of the water hole, and attached it to the page with an accordian of folded paper (Figure 4–12, C). "I want to make it look like it will swing and make waves right off the paper."

Kelly was in control of the conventions she chose to use. Although she wanted to continue to depict the movement that was essential to her story, she decided not to continue with pop-ups. She explained, "You're gonna see what happens to the water hole on the next page. But the rest of the book is going to be flat on the page. No more pop-ups."

But it wasn't until she shared the story with the class the next day that I saw her metaphor. First, she read the pages I had already heard and seen, then concluded with, "The water hole is going to be hopped on" (Figure 4–12, D). Above the words is a picture of the sled driver, legs outstretched, atop a recently released coiled spring—a perfect metaphor to show that the water hole indeed can't escape being hopped on now!

The other children were impressed with this solution, too, offering comments like "I like the part where the water hole is about to get hopped on" and "I like the part where you was just gonna hop on the hole" (field notes, October 15, 1987).

Figure 4–12   Kelly's Sled Dog Story

a

b

c

d

Action Lines

The use of action lines is another convention many of the children used to show motion and movement. In a sense, this convention was used as a kind of metaphor as well. Notice, for example, the swirling, stylized lines that Paul used to show the rolling snowballs in Figure 4–13.

Figure 4–13   Paul's Snowballs

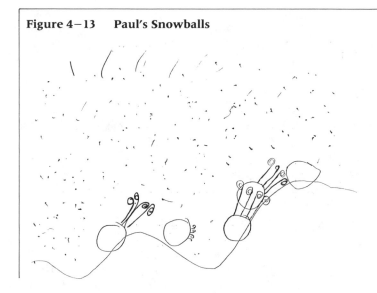

Graham also used lines to represent the path his sled had just taken as it flew down the hill (Figure 4–14). "I bumped into a stump," he explained. "I did *not* like it. See, I hit the stump and I went right up. Here's the ground level. . . . It got so much speed!" Then, Graham explained his other use of lines in this picture. "These lines, they show you're going fast!"

Figure 4–14   Graham's Sled Story

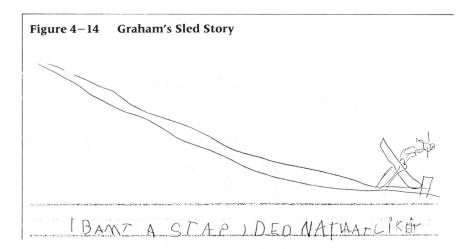

In our Western culture, movement, especially of figures, is frequently accentuated by lines, or sometimes a blur, even though real movement doesn't produce these effects. This is especially evident in cartoons, which are a daily part of children's environment, and television, book illustrations, and newspapers.

Some theorists, such as Kepes (1969), argue that these metaphors for movement are really imitations of photographic effects, citing examples of moving objects taken by cameras with the shutter open for a longer period of time. This creates an effect of movement: a blur next to the object. But others, such as Sarah Friedman and Marguerite Stevenson (1980), argue that these action lines were used long before the invention of the camera, tracing their use as far back as the twelfth century.

Gombrich (1980), in his article "Standards of Truth: The Arrested Image and the Moving Eye," discusses the differences between machine-made and man-made images and argues that even "factual images," like photos of lightning or X-rays, must be interpreted by the viewer. There must be agreed-upon conventions in order to communicate meaning. Gombrich shares a cartoon from *Punch* to illustrate the problem:

The desperate artist in Smilby's picture [Figure 4–15]...is shown wrestling with the need to produce what I have called in my title an "arrested image" of his view through the window during a thunderstorm. As he is trying to make a truthful record of the flashes of lightning which race across the sky, we can see his hand swishing from one position to another, for Smilby in his turn is presented with the task of representing movement in a "still." (p. 181)

Examples of the use of the lines and blurred images cartoonists like Smilby employ to show movement appeared throughout the children's work, and when I would ask them how they got the idea, they usually related it to having seen it somewhere in their environment. Some, like Kelly or Paul, would respond with answers like, "You know, like you see in books," while others were more specific. Ming, for example, told me she got the idea from Bugs Bunny and Road Runner cartoons, while Sarah brought in a Frosty the Snowman story to show me a specific example.

Sally decided, quite on her own, to show *how* cartoons can show movement, as part of her book "How to Make

---

Figure 4—15   Smilby, Drawing from *Punch* (February 1, 1956, p. 177)

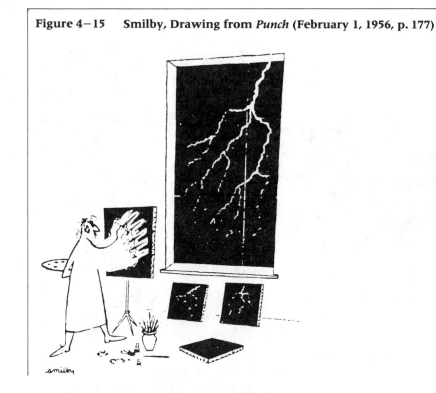

Cartoons" (Figure 4—16). On one page (Figure 4—16, B) she showed multiple figures, use of different postures, and, of course, action lines as her cartoon figure flips the pillow in the air. The others in the class were supportive of Sally's attempts, telling her, for example, that they liked how she showed how to make a bird. But they were also critical.

Gwen challenged, "Why didn't you name it 'How to Make Pictures,' 'cause if you wanted it to be like cartoons, you would have to make pop-ups so it would move."

Sally defended her book, citing the page shown in Figure 4—16, B, stating that she showed with stick figures how "you can make them do things and stuff."

But other children agreed with Gwen, saying Sally shouldn't call it cartoons, "'cause cartoons *really* move." Ming suggested that if she wanted a cartoon book, it would need to

Figure 4–16   Sally's Book "How to Make Cartoons"

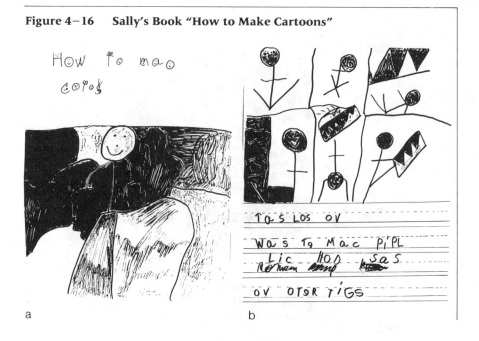

a   b

be a flip book to show things moving.

In discussing this group's conference later, Pat and I marveled at the difference in the understanding of the term *cartoon*. For us, comic books and political cartoons fit well in the definition of cartoon, but most of the children think differently: they equate cartoons with the action-packed moving cartoons on television. The importance of the electronic as well as the print media has had a profound effect on the conventions for symbolizing movement in these children's literacy experience. And, as Gwen suggested, it may be the clue to the widespread popularity of pop-up books in this first-grade classroom.

Pop-Ups

Early in the school year, Megan shared the draft of her dog story—a story that was to have a profound effect on the writing and drawing in the class. Before she turned to the last page, she prepared her classmates for something a little different.

Figure 4-17   Megan's Pop-Up

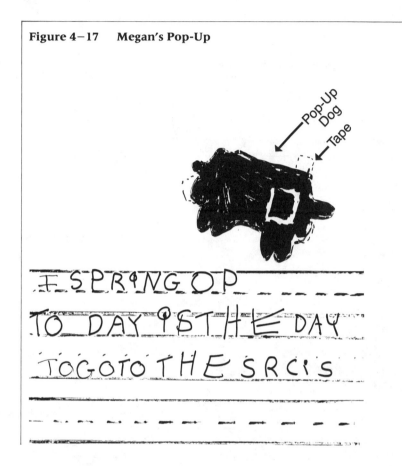

"This is something special," she told them, then showed the page (Figure 4—17). "That thing's supposed to pop up. 'I spring up,'" she read to the class. "'Today is the day I go to the circus.'"

Murmurs of interest spread through her audience.

"Why I said it came up is because in the book, he's supposed to, like, *spring* up. See?" she demonstrated. "It's supposed to spring out like this, 'cept it won't right now, I have to fix it."

It didn't take long for this convention to spread through the class. From the beginning, it intrigued the children with its possibilities for showing movement and extending the

Figure 4–18   The Spread of Megan's Content and Conventions

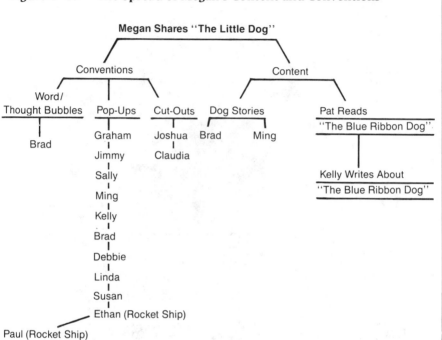

limits of the static page. In mid-October, I documented the spread of this convention through the class (see Figure 4–18). And as the year progressed, it became an accepted classroom convention for showing movement, used or attempted at least once by every child in the class by January. (This does not include the two new class members who arrived after November.)

Why did the use of the pop-up convention take such a strong hold in this particular classroom? First of all, I believe, because it was done well, and *it worked* to show movement. Children followed Megan's lead, but used their pop-ups in very different ways, rejecting them when they didn't work and modifying them to suit their particular communication needs. Paul, for example, didn't try pop-ups until he was in the midst of a space story, and he decided it would help him show the spaceship moving through space (Figure 4–19).

Figure 4–19   Paul's Space Story

"10−9−8−7−6−5−4−3−2−1. Blast off! Boom!" Paul read to me, then showed me how you can actually lift the spaceship and fly it through the air to the planet at the top of the page (Figure 4−19, A).

"But then," he turned the page and read, "'The rocket ship exploded'" (Figure 4−19, B). He pointed to all the shapes on the page. "That's all the pieces that broke up and some are falling."

He stopped to explain his plans before going on. "This time, I'm gonna make a new spaceship, and it's not gonna explode—it's gonna go up and see aliens"—which is just what he proceeded to communicate on the last page of his story (Figure 4−19, C).

Paul's use of pop-ups is illustrative of the children's selective use of this convention—when it would work for a particular situation. Paul found it useful to use on two pages of his story to show how the rocket flew through space. But he used a different kind of metaphor, geometric shapes scattered on the page, to represent the explosion.

Often, the pop-ups were used as part of the solution. Words and picture pop-ups each contributed to communicating the movement the children had in mind.

Words and Pictures

Right from the beginning, Megan used pop-ups in conjunction with verbs to show action. In her first story, it was as if the verb "spring" didn't communicate strongly enough what she had in mind, so she added the pop-up of the dog springing up (Figure 4−17). In the same story she used both words and pictures on another page to represent the motion (Figure 4−20). "I love to jump over rocks," says the little dog. And Megan drew him in a frozen moment in the midst of his jump to *show* as well as *tell* the action. She seemed to feel a need to illustrate the verbs in her stories.

Like Megan, Kelly also relied on words, especially strong verbs, with her pictures. One morning, she sat down to write about a bus accident that many of the children had witnessed. She began with a picture, with part of the bus shown, the tree it crashed into, and a loud exploding sound, "BANG!" (Figure 4−21). Then she wrote the words "The bus crashing into a tree."

Figure 4–20   Megan's Dog

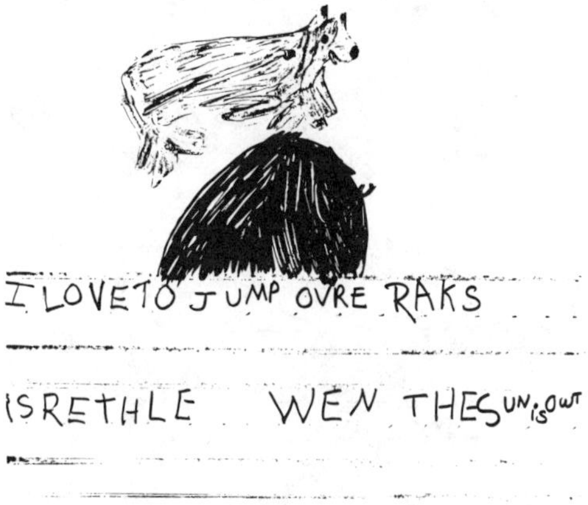

I LOVE TO JUMP OVRE RAKS

IS RETHLE   WEN THE SUN IS OUT

Figure 4–21   Kelly's Bus Crash

THE BUS CRRHCHING

INTO A TREE.

Figure 4–22   Kelly's Volcano

Unlike Megan, who often wrote first, then illustrated her words, Kelly first drew the movement of the crash, then felt the need to further explain her picture with words.

Although Kelly's vocabulary was quite sophisticated, she continued to rely on pictures to complete the whole story in most of her writing. Her adventure story is another example. "While I was watching my sun, a volcano erupted behind me," she wrote. "Choke," the volcano sputters in her picture as the lava pours out behind her (Figure 4–22).

Kelly didn't always draw first, then write. Often, she want back and forth between the words and the pictures. One day she began by writing the words "I am at Debbie's trailer," then drew the picture of herself approaching Debbie's door. Dissatisfied, she added another sentence with a more precise verb to show the action she wanted to communicate: "Another way to say it is, I arrived at Debbie's trailer" (Figure 4–23).

Figure 4–23   Kelly at Debbie's Trailer

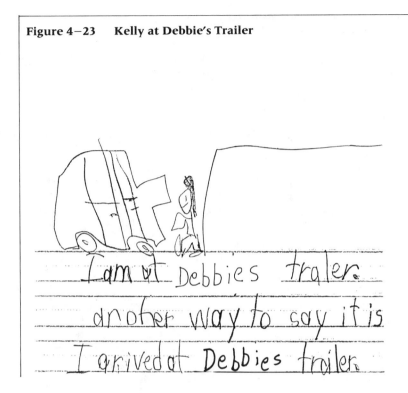

I am at Debbies traler.

another way to say it is

I arrived at Debbies trailer.

These are all examples from the children's self-selected topics. They wrote about things they chose to communicate to others. How do these modes of expressing movement transfer to other areas of the curriculum? To gain a picture of how the class showed pieces of the action on a similar topic, we'll turn once again to the Rotten Jack journals.

Motion in Rotten Jack

As the children made daily observations in their "What Happened to Rotten Jack" journals, they used many symbols to depict the important elements of motion they observed. In Table 4–1 I have categorized the different modes I found in these science journals.

Table 4−1   Rotten Jack: Symbols for Movement

	Multiple Images	"As It Happens"	Frozen Moment	Metaphor	Action Lines	Pop-ups	Words & Pictures
Brad							■
Ming			■				■
Kelly							■
Nick		■			■		■
Joshua					■		
Eugene				■			■
Debbie		■		■			■
Ethan							■
Gwen		■			■		■
TJ							■
Julie				■			■
Jimmy		■		■			■
Sally					■		■
Paul				■			■
Claudia	■						■
Sarah	■				■		■
Megan	■	■					■
Susan		■					■
Graham	■	■	■		■		■
Ashley			■	■			■
Bruce		■			■		■
Linda		■					■

Figure 4−24 shows one example from each category. Megan used multiple images as she speculated on what caused the pumpkin to fall: "I think the top fell in. The pumpkin was squooshed" (Figure 4−24, A). Jimmy used swirling scribbling motions to symbolize the motion of the pumpkin falling: "Rotten Jack falls down" (Figure 4−24, B). The frozen moment of action that Ashley decided she needed to communicate was a little different; she wanted to depict the hovering flies that were attracted to the rotting vegetable: "Rotten Jack is attracting flies" (Figure 4−24, C). Some of the children, like Eugene, used the metaphor of stylized geometric shapes pointing out in different directions to represent the moment of collapse: "Jack fell apart" (Figure 4−24, D). Sally relied heavily on her audience's understanding of action lines to show Jack tipping over. Her picture finished the text she began with "Jack is. . ." (Figure 4−24, E). Sarah, on the

Figure 4–24 **Symbols for Movement. A: Megan—Multiple Images. B: Jimmy—As It Happens. C: Ashley—Frozen Moment. D: Eugene—Metaphor. E: Sally—Action Lines. F: Sarah—Words and Pictures.**

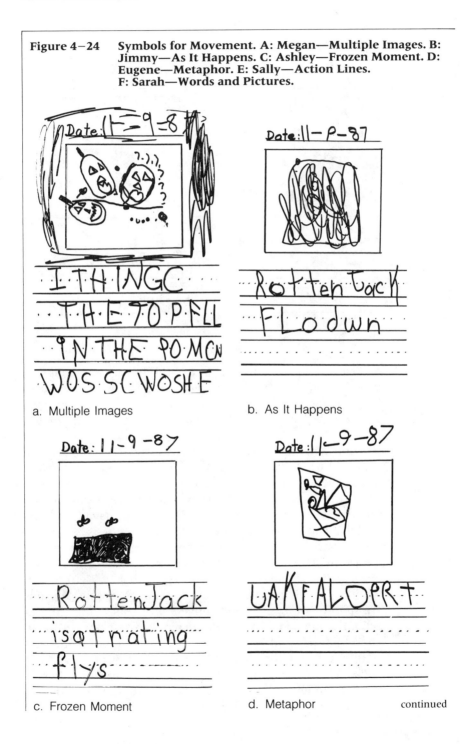

a. Multiple Images

b. As It Happens

c. Frozen Moment

d. Metaphor   continued

Figure 4–24   Continued

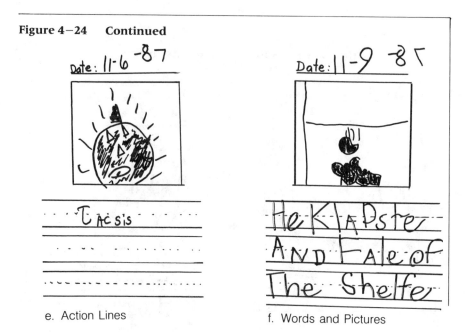

e. Action Lines   f. Words and Pictures

other hand, like twenty-one out of the twenty-two children, relied on words as well as her pictures to tell the whole story: "He collapsed and fell off the shelf," she wrote. She used strong verbs along with other symbols to illustrate the movement in picture form (Figure 4–24, F).

And what about the pop-ups used by every child in the course of their daily writing? Not one child chose to transfer this convention to the science journals. I can only speculate about the reasons for this. They might have assumed that they weren't supposed to, although it would have been perfectly acceptable to Pat if they had. My hypothesis is that the children used pop-ups, as I demonstrated above, because they *worked* in those situations to show movement. The motion most of the children wanted to depict in their Rotten Jack writing was the motion of falling down or collapsing. Pop-ups are simply not a very good convention to show this kind of action, while some of the other modes were. Interestingly, almost all the children relied on a combination of words and pictures to show some kind of movement. This points out the flexibility and versatility of the children's use of different symbols—and symbol systems—to communicate motion.

Conclusion

Throughout history, men and women have tried to suggest motion on a static surface. Some have relied primarily on the printed word to call up memory images of past experiences. Motion is conveyed through strong verbs and sensory indicators, like crashing or whirring sounds. Even young children rely on these techniques. They incorporate words like "bang" or "choke" into their pictures, or use lots of action words like Megan's "springing" or Paul's "exploded."

Others have relied on pictures to indicate movement. Artists like Tintoretto, Goya, and Michaelangelo were masters at showing the strains that actions put on the body, elongating and stretching figures, or showing the facial distortions that appear when people force their bodies into action. They created the kinds of symbols that would work to communicate motion for their particular purposes.

And so do the children. They create metaphors like Graham's angry New York car biting at his heels; freeze frogs flying through the air; and create pop-ups to make the water seem to splash out of the pages of the book. They are skillful interpreters of a movement-filled world, able to translate in their own ways the pieces of the action that are a part of their world.

chapter five

There's More than Black and White in the Palette of Literacy: Children's Use of Color

Close your eyes for a moment and imagine a simple scene: Picture yourself taking a fresh lemon and slowly cutting it in half on a cutting board. What do you see and feel? Most people report a vivid image of the texture, smell, and, above all, color of the lemon. And when they try to *communicate* rich mental images, people often rely on references to color to bring an important dimension to their literacy. Children, too, are aware of the importance of color in transferring their images, memories, and stories through the page to others around them.

As Kelly wrote about her visit to Debbie's trailer, she was seeing colorful pictures in her mind. "I'm seeing Debbie's trailer, and I'm seeing that it's bright silver, and I'm seeing Debbie playing outside," she explained to me as she worked one morning. Her use of black and gray crayons to try to transfer that silver color to the page was not random, but a deliberate testing out of what colors would work best to communicate her picture of Debbie's trailer.

In reviewing the body of research relating to children's use of color, I was struck by the absence of any mention of the child's intentions—of what his or her purpose for using the colors might be. In fact, the experiments meant to test color usage ignore that factor altogether. Ambrose Corcoran (1954), for example, hypothesized that preschool children use colors "in the exact order of presentation" (p. 106). To test this claim, he set up four colors in a trough in front of an easel and asked the children to paint. He found that twelve out of nineteen children used the colors in the trough in a left to right progression "at least once out of two turns at the easel." Based on these scant results, he concluded that "the mode of painting is to apply the color without conscious deliberation" (p. 113).

In another rather bizarre study, experimenters Carol and Edward Lawler (1965) presented young children with mimeographed sketches of a girl wearing a dress and read them two three-sentence stories about the girl, one happy and one sad. The children were then shown two crayons, one yellow and one brown, and asked which of the two colors the girl's dress should be when she was happy and which when she was sad. Their results and conclusions? "Significant trends showing brown associated with a sad mood and yellow associated with a happy mood were found....The fact that preschool children who have been subjected to relatively little cultural conditioning have strong color-mood associations similar to those found in adults gives some support to Guilford's theory that color choices are biologically determined" (p. 31).

Both of these studies suffer from limitations that are common to the study of children's abilities. The most severe limitation is the context, or lack of it, for these studies. The children are given tasks to perform for adult experimenters. Not only do they have no previous experience with these adults, but their options are severely limited in how they can respond to the tasks they are given. These researchers set up their experiments in order to prove, or perhaps disprove, their pre-existing assumptions, then drew far-reaching conclusions from those contrived studies.

But when children are working to communicate ideas that they want to share with others, they experiment to add texture and dimension to their literacy. Their explorations are not random, however. Because they find that color helps them to communicate, they use it consciously and intentionally. The following three scenes from Pat McLure's classroom illustrate how children consciously use color:

Ming couldn't find the exact color she needed one morning and had to mix green and brown. She explained to me, "This, is my hand all muddy-green-green mud from working in the dirt. You can tell by the color."

Paul hummed as he drew a picture of himself, then frowned, "The markers are running out." He switched to crayon, then explained how he would color his hair. "I better use yellow for my hair, 'cause it's sort of yellowish blonde. If you use yellow and put pencil very lightly, it looks like dirty-blonde hair."

"I'm drawing me watching the hermit crabs," Kelly told me. "But my eyes are really hazel, not blue. I couldn't find a good crayon for hazel. I'm gonna draw my hair darker, too. All the blondes look too yellowish, and I was gonna save yellow for the skin."

In these examples, the children were all consciously experimenting with the medium—discovering what it can and can't do to help communicate their messages. They were also quite aware that colors aren't viewed in isolation, but that they influence each other. In the example above, Kelly knew that using shades of yellow for skin and hair wouldn't work, and on another day, she consciously chose a pencil to do the title on her red cover, explaining to me, "I want this for my title. On the red, when you write with a pencil, it looks like gold shines."

Other children experimented with actually mixing colors and recording it. Gwen told me she got the idea to do her book "A Book about Colors" because "Sarah was working on colors, somebody else was writing about shapes, so I just thought about it."

"There are a lot of different colors in the world," reads the first page of her book, with globes of color arranged above. On many of the pages, she records her experiments mixing colors.

"I tested them out," she explained, showing me the sheet of paper, full of colorful crayon scribbles, where she had tried combining different colors before putting them in her book for later reference and use.

Categories for the Use of Color

Color for Detail

The major reason that the children used color in this first-grade classroom was to help communicate their detailed observations; they often needed to record and share with others certain details that could best be communicated with color representations. The following excerpt from my field notes (September 22, 1987) shows the care that Ming took as she, with Claudia's help, worked on a page of her "friends book."

[*Claudia is directing Ming on the coloring of Pat's pants.*]
Claudia: Black for pants.
Ming: Don't worry. If I make a mistake, I have myself to blame.
Claudia: Why?
Ming: 'Cause it's my picture. Gotta make her head now.
Claudia: Black.
Ming: Kinda black and white mixed. [*Draws and colors.*] Claudia, you come over to my house sometime?

Claudia: Why?

Ming: Play.... You gotta watch out for my brother. Now [*to Ruth*] you. You have a blue skirt, arms, make your hands in back. What color socks? [*She looks and keeps up a running commentary as she draws.*] Brown, brown, brown, hair. OK, now. [*Gets up and goes over to take a look at Brenda. Returns and sits down to work, black crayon in hand.*] Now, black dress...

Claudia: Black, yes.

[*Brian walks by.*]

Ming [*to Brian*]: I might put you in my book. [*Thinks about it as he walks away.*] No, no boys in this book. [*She draws and talks.*] A bunch of flowers on her shirt and green leafs.... Gotta make a face... [*Scoots down on the floor to see Brenda's tights. Claudia goes and checks, too.*]

Claudia: Black shoes!

Ming: Blonde hair. [*Starts to color it in with orangish-blonde crayon.*]

Claudia: No! Not... it white! You forget her shoes!

Ming: I'll make her shoes last.

Over a month later, Claudia was writing about a trip to the apple orchard with the class and was carefully drawing herself with the teacher. She made many conscious decisions concerning color—the tools that would best convey the colors she wanted to use, and a compromise between what Pat was actually wearing and what Claudia *likes* her teacher to wear, as this excerpt from my field notes (November 10, 1987) shows:

Claudia: Now, I make what she wear today. [*Hums.*]

Ruth: Claudia looks happy in the picture.

Claudia: Teacher does, too.

Ruth: So does Mrs. McLure. Yup.

Claudia: Like my teacher dress. I'm drawin'...'cause....

Ruth: So you have pants on, and Mrs. McLure has a dress on.

Claudia: Yes. [*Laughs.*] OK, I no color—what my teacher has...

Ruth: Oh, what she has on today?

Claudia: Oh, blue.... This a pencil.... I try this one, this a pencil.

Ruth: This is kinda red....

Claudia: Now, blue. Yes!

Ruth: Oh, I see. She does have both these colors on today, doesn't she?

Claudia: Mmm. Her pants black?

Ruth: I think so.

Claudia: Oh, no, this color.

Ruth: Oh, brown?

Claudia: Yes, this color. No, my teacher. . .yesterday. Yesterday.

Ruth: Those were the clothes she had on yesterday?

Claudia: No, the day. . .I no like, I no like when my teacher wear this. . .black.

The details the children represented with color were not all related to people, however. Kelly, for example, created in her book about butterflies careful drawings using, as she assured me, "only the colors butterflies can really be." And Ming, in her first published book, "The Little Red Car," used changes in color to show how the car faded as it aged. In her explanation as she read the book to me, she stressed that it was important that the last car is a different color. "It looks different 'cause it's *older*."

Cultural and Symbolic Effects of Color

Colors are seen, felt, used, and responded to in our everyday lives; there is no escaping how meaning laden colors become for both adults and children. Hans and Shulamith Kreitler (1972) write, "In daily life, colors are bound up with forms, objects, meanings, situations, memories, any or all of which may determine the pleasure or displeasure we feel when seeing colors" (p. 33).

Originally, I had identified two separate categories for the cultural and symbolic effects of color in the children's writing and drawing, but as I read the literature, I found the two inextricably related. Culturally shared meanings are often tied to the semiotics of a situation and can change very quickly in a culture. Two experiments on associations to color serve as striking examples. In the first experiment (Kreitler 1956), performed in 1941 in Jerusalem, yellow proved to be an extremely unpleasant color for most of the subjects (86 percent), as it reminded them of the "yellow patch of the Jews." On the other hand, blue appeared to be an optimistic color of hope for 72 percent of the subjects, since the "'blue shirt,' the popular uniform in Palestine at that time, stood for generally shared hopes for a national revival for a socialist and brotherly society" (Kreitler & Kreitler, 1972, p. 60).

In an interesting repetition of this experiment on another

generation of Israelis in 1960, the results were very different. This time, there was a great preference for yellow as the color of the reviving desert in the country (41 percent), but almost no (3 percent) association of blue with hope (Kreitler & Elblinger, 1961).*

An example a little closer to home is the deliberate change of the colors in fast-food chains in America. A decade ago, bright reds, blues, and oranges represented "new, fast, and efficient" for restaurant chains like McDonald's and Burger King. In the late eighties, these chains are purposefully changing their colors to those that represent health to their consumers—notably browns and greens. (Next time you drive by a Burger King, notice that their traditional orange roofs are quickly being converted to brown!)

Colors and emotions are intimately related, and both the visual and verbal languages reflect that relationship. There are many metaphoric references to color: some people are said to "see the world through rose-colored glasses," have a "colorful background," or "get the blues." On the visual side, Stern (1955) contends that in Western culture, "a strong attraction to or revulsion from the blue colors is characteristic of introverted and emotionally highly controlled individuals, while a fascination with red suggests aggressive impulses." (Based on the Kreitler experiments in Israel, however, this may only a reflection of our culture in the 1950s and may no longer be true today.)

For the six- and seven-year-old children I observed, color is also meaning laden. For Claudia, purple is a color that shows happiness. She was pleased to see herself included in Ming's "friend book" and watched as Ming carefully drew Claudia in the black and yellow outfit she was wearing. She looked at the drawing of herself and smiled. "I smile. Happy."

---

* Three of the research studies quoted here are cited by Kreitler & Kreitler (1972) and were unavailable to me in the original, either unpublished or untranslated. The three sources are: H. Kreitler (1956), *Psychologische grundlagen des kunstgenusses*, unpublished doctoral dissertation, University of Graz, Austria; H. Kreitler and S. Eblinger (1961), *Tension and relief of colors and color combinations*, unpublished manuscript, Tel Aviv University; and E. Stern (1955), *Die tests in die klinischen psychologie*, Zurich: Rascher Verlag.

She reached into the crayon box, found what she was looking for, and carefully colored in her own face purple (Figure 5−1).

Sometimes the color meanings derive from the larger culture. One example is Eugene's fascinating drawing depicting the end of the day (Figure 5−2). (This example actually represents all the visual dimensions children use: time, space, movement, and color.) Eugene explained what he meant to show on this page. "See, the day is over. That's some of the light from the moon, and it comes out as this light." He pointed to the lines reflecting off the car. "A tree's in front of the moon," he went on. "This is a big harvest moon. That's why it's orange, or you wouldn't know it was fall. And the moon shows that the day is over. Sometimes I watch the moon and the falling stars with Paul—that's my dad." To Eugene, a big orange moon was a symbol of the autumn season. He didn't need to say that it was fall because he assumed that his audience shared the same cultural meaning for an orange moon. Ming also had a cultural sense about color. She knew that her audience would associate the color blue with water, even though water is often colorless. In her flower story, she explained about her "fancy watering can." "This is the watering can," she told me. "I wanted to make it fancy. It's glass, so you can see the water inside. Blue water." She looked up at me from her coloring to explain, "You can tell there's water in it, so I made it blue."

This use of color may be a learned convention. Many of the books that surround Ming and the other children do use blue to represent water. Linda used another color convention in her apple story, and again, I can only speculate that she has learned this from the books she has seen and read. As she drew and colored in her "fake apple that you can eat," she carefully made white semicircles on the side of the red apple. "These are the shines on the apple," she explained. "They almost make it look like it's smiling!"

These children were learning the uses of color in the books that were read to them and that they read themselves. In an interesting conversation between Sarah and Sally early in September, I was able to observe them as they struggled, and ultimately came to terms with, the use of black line drawings with some watercolor tints in an illustrated Snow White story.

Figure 5–1
Ming's Friend
Claudia

Figure 5–2
Eugene's Drawing:
"The Day Is Over"

Mississippi

The
Mississippi
river

a

the Mississippi
river in a sto
rom.

b

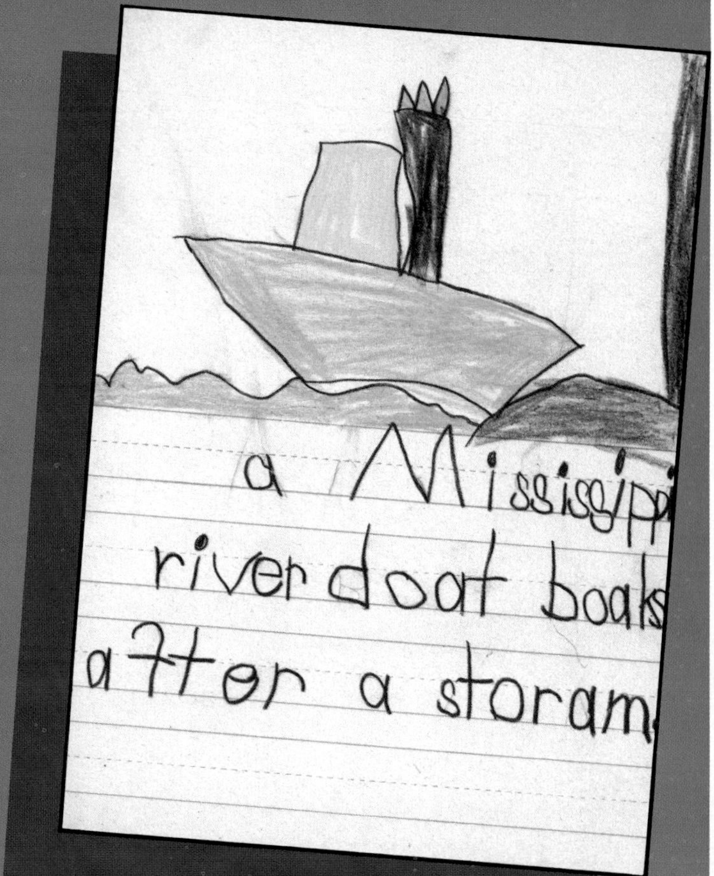

a Mississippi river boat boats after a storam.

c

Figure 5–3 Kelly's Mississippi River Story

Figure 5–4
Ming's Rainbow

I Love robos
Tar Kom From
LiT AND rAN Gn
BAY Tr LiT @ GONG
INGToTORERAN@HSKArSAroboS

itwraitmoing

Figure 5–5
TJ's Rain

"This story is pretty much the same as mine at home, but the pictures are real different," Sarah told Sally. "Her lips..." she pointed to the cover picture of Snow White, "should be more red. See, they're pale here, not real red."

She flipped through the book, and together, she and Sally scrutinized the lips on each illustration of Snow White. "They're black here," Sarah shook her head, "and black again, and again."

The illustrations on these pages were mostly outlined— Snow White's lips drawn in black, but never filled in with color. Although I would not have interpreted these lips as black, clearly Sarah and Sally did.

Sally was adamant. "Her lips should be red. Red like in the movie."

But Sarah kept trying to figure out what the illustrator had in mind. "They're always black here, though." She looked closely, and pondered for a minute. "They're not really black inside; they're actually white inside."

"They're just supposed to be pale, then, I guess. Like on the cover," Sally decided.

The Influence of Light

Just as the children worked out the culturally shared conventions for the uses of color, they also observed the world around them and found that lighting has a strong effect on how colors are perceived.

When Kelly worked on her Mississippi River story (Figure 5–3—also discussed in Chapter 2), the use of color was extremely important to her, as indicated in the following excerpt from my field notes (September 28, 1987):

Kelly: This will be the shore here, and there always has to be water for the river.... See that? The boat. It's a steamboat. The brown is for the land. [*Takes a blue crayon.*] This is the water.

Ruth: Seems like you draw in pencil, then color it in.

Kelly: Yeah, so I know how to color it, and it also helps me to remember what to write there. *See, the different pages, the steamboat is always different colors. It fades into different colors by the rain* [italics mine].

Without Kelly's explanation as she worked, I would never have known how deliberate her color changes were in this story. She chose to represent the reflection of the light as it changed through a storm.

Many adult artists, both writers and painters, are also concerned with the effect of light on colors. Consider, for example, the contemporaries Baudelaire and Delacroix, nineteenth-century giants in the world of poetry and art. Delacroix was a noted colorist, who worked to create the impression of light as it occurred in nature, mixing colors so that his audience would see no isolated colors, only the blurring of color lines that light creates. He was known for omitting black from his palette because light always modifies it to another color.

Baudelaire was an ardent admirer of Delacroix, writing analyses, as well as poetic odes, to his works. In Baudelaire's salon reviews of Delacroix's paintings, he stresses above all the painter's "unprecedented achievement in harmonizing colour" (Abel, 1980, p. 47).

This same harmonious light-reflecting atmosphere is important in Baudelaire's writing. But, as various critics have pointed out, he uses color words only rarely. "Rather than literally adapting painterly techniques, Baudelaire chooses images that evoke a harmonious atmosphere. One striking aspect of Baudelaire's poetry is the frequency with which he uses imagery of sunshine (one critic has calculated that Baudelaire uses the word 'soleil' sixty-three times in 'Les Fleurs du Mal,' making it fifth in order of frequency), especially of sunlight diffused at sunset or through mist in such a way that it dissolves a scene into a flow of refracted light" (Abel, 1980, p. 50).

Although the children in Pat McLure's class used color words, much of their writing, as well as drawing, about color was in terms of light. Ming was writing about rainbows one day (a topic many first-grade teachers come to dread) and was working out information she had learned about the light of rainbows.

"I love rainbows," she read to me (Figure 5—4). "They come from light and raindrops by their light going together in the raindrops. It 'aflects' a rainbow."

Megan was the first to appreciate and comment on TJ's representation of the effects of light on color in the atmosphere. Her favorite page of his "School Story" was the page that read, "It was raining the next morning" (Figure 5—5).

"I like the way you made the rain different colors," she commented.

"You mean...um...you mean you like that part in the color right there?" he asked, pointing to a corner of the picture. "That was the sun trying to come out a little bit. It looks crazy like a meteor."

Megan nodded, "I like the rain...like...."

"You mean right there? I added blue, green, yellow, and stuff to make it that color," he explained. "The way how I did the rain was I took the point and I slided down and stuff."

Claudia, too, both writes and draws about the effects of light or, in some cases, the absence of it. One day, as I sat next to her during writing time, she drew her cat Mathilda with an orange crayon. When she finished, she took out a black crayon and drew a dark streak across the page.

"Night!" she exclaimed, then proceeded to color in the whole page with a black crayon, covering even the cat drawing.

"My cat likes night," she said aloud slowly, as she wrote the letters *M, C, L, N.*

Claudia is also fascinated by the use of colors in the books she reads, and especially the conventions for showing light illuminated in dark areas. During reading time early in the year, Claudia was looking at a picture book about Pinocchio, a book that had been read to her at home. She thought it was very funny, she told me, that some of the pictures have "paint" (are colored) and others don't.

"Some paint...maybe people paint," she muttered as she looked through the pictures. "He fall down." She pointed to the tear on his face. "He cry." Then she came to the part where the characters in the story are in the fish's stomach. In the picture, there is a table with a lighted candle, illuminating just the area around the table.

"Light? Light? Why? Light in tummy? Why?" She turned to Kelly. "Look. This light. Why a light in tummy?"

Kelly looked up, glanced at the picture, and responded, "That *is* silly."

Claudia picked up the book and brought it to her friend Ming. "Look! Look at light."

Ming, however, was more interested in her own reading and merely shrugged, keeping her eyes glued to her book.

Undaunted, Claudia continued to try to find people to share this strange picture with. "Mrs. McLure! Look at light in tummy!"

From this careful look at the children writing and reading, I learned that a colorful palette appears to add a dimension to the children's literacy in three main ways: it records the details they have observed, it acts as a cultural or symbolic representation, and it shows the effects of light.

Color in Rotten Jack

When I turned once again to the Rotten Jack journals, this time to analyze the classwide use of color, I expected to find the three main categories that stood out so clearly in the children's other writing and drawing. And I did. Just as in other areas of the curriculum, when the children turned their efforts to recording their observations of the pumpkin, they used color for detail, for symbolic representation, and for showing the effects of light. But I also noticed some differences. Table 5−1 summarizes the classwide use of color in the different categories.

I found much more use of actual color words, like *orange, black, red,* or *brown.* In fact, eighteen out of twenty-two children in the class relied on these color words—as well as color pictures—to record their observations. Only four children used color in their pictures with no words to enhance those important color aspects.

Figure 5−6 shows examples from each of the classwide categories. "Rotten Jack has brown spots around his eyes and nose and mouth," writes Paul. He recorded the brown detail with both his colored crayon and the word "brown" (Figure 5−6, A). In the same category, Sarah illustrates in her picture the words "There is white fuzz on the skin" (Figure 5−6, B). Graham explained to me a page from his science journal where he uses color symbolically. "Jack is wet," he wrote, and colored in a blue puddle within Jack's mouth (Figure 5−6, C). "There's water," he explained. "I drew it blue to show it was wet. It wasn't really blue, though. Just wet." Brian surprised me by comparing Jack's state of decomposition to the effects of firelight. "He has like it was in a fire," he wrote, and showed the colorful, dancing flames engulfing the pumpkin (Figure 5−6, D).

Table 5−1   Rotten Jack: Symbols for Color

	Detail	Cultural and Symbolic	Light	Color Metaphor
Brad	■		■	■
Ming	■			■
Kelly	■			
Nick	■			
Joshua	■			
Eugene	■			
Debbie	■			
Ethan	■			
Gwen	■	■		
TJ	■			
Julie	■			
Jimmy	■			
Sally	■			
Paul	■			
Claudia	■			
Sarah	■			■
Megan	■			
Susan	■			
Graham	■	■		■
Ashley	■	■		
Bruce	■			
Linda	■			

Other children throughout the class made comparisons based on color, which called for a new category: the use of color metaphors. Figure 5−6 shows two examples from this category. When Sarah tried to record how Jack looked after he fell, she reached for a metaphor: "He looks like orange mashed potatoes" (Figure 5−6, E). Graham, too, wanted to compare the powdery substance he observed on the pumpkin to another white substance his audience would be familiar with: "Jack is getting powder—it looks like salt," he recorded (Figure 5−6, F). The demands of this science task—with its emphasis on careful observation—seemed to call for the use of metaphors, particularly those related to color in the children's literacy.

Figure 5–6   **Symbols for Color. A: Paul—Detail. B: Sarah—Detail. C: Graham—Cultural and Symbolic. D: Brian—Light. E: Sarah—Color Metaphor. F: Graham—Color Metaphor.**

Date: 1-6-87

rot ten Jack Hest brown sPots (rewND HesI Y AND NosAND MowTH

a. Detail

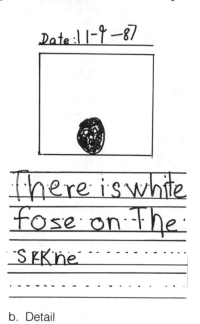

Date: 11-9-87

There is white fose on The SRKne

b. Detail

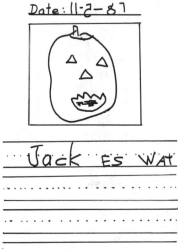

Date: 11-2-87

Jack ES WAt

c. Cultural and Symbolic

Date:

he Hos llic It wus inu fir

d. Light

continued

Figure 5–6   Continued

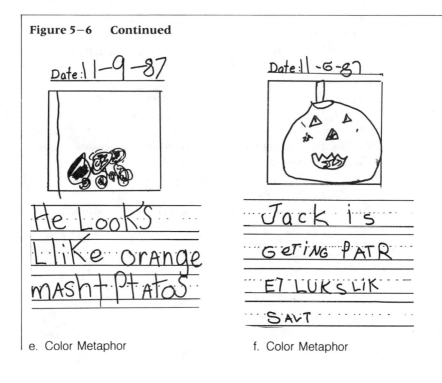

e. Color Metaphor   f. Color Metaphor

Conclusion

Recording and communicating color and light is an important, though often ignored, dimension of literacy. William Bragg writes, "Light, therefore, using the full meaning of the word, transmits energy which is the mainstay of life, and gives to living beings the power of observation" (Kepes, 1969, p. 134).

The six- and seven-year-old children in Pat McLure's first-grade classroom use this power of observation to integrate words and pictures to communicate messages. And color helps them represent significant details, symbolize the happiness of a certain mood, communicate the effects of light, and even create metaphors that help to share an observation. But it isn't only children who integrate words and pictures as they wrestle with depicting color. Think of Baudelaire's use of sunlight, or the struggles of novelist Sherwood Anderson, who wrote, "There was a kind of painting I was seeking in my prose, word to be laid against word in just a certain way, a kind of word color, an arch of words and sentences, the color to be squeezed out of simple words, simple sentence construction" (Hjerter, 1986, p. 78).

Children need more than the black-and-white page—or the purple-and-white mimeograph paper—to communicate their messages. Poet and artist Antoine de Saint-Exupéry reminds us: "It is impossible to survive on refrigerators, politics, balance sheets, and crossword puzzles, you see! It is impossible! It is impossible to live without poetry and *color* and love" (Foulke, 1956; from a letter to "General X," left in his barracks room the day Saint-Exupéry disappeared in his plane).

chapter six

Dimensions of Literacy: Conclusions and Implications

[Language] is a tool because with it we order our experience, matching the data abstracted from the flux about us with linguistic units: words, phrases, sentences. What is true of verbal languages is also true of visual "languages": we match the data from the flux of visual experience with image-cliches, with stereotypes of one kind or another, according to the way we have been taught to see.

S. I. Hayakawa

Children use both verbal and visual languages as tools to help them sort out, understand, and cope with their world. As they become acculturated to the concepts that guide the society they live in, they rely on these languages, or inner symbol systems, that they create. Children use and refine these inner systems when they are involved in literacy events—learning ways to translate and communicate them onto the limited dimensions of a page.

The preceeding chapters have dealt with the key dimensions I found children to be coping with as part of their literacy acquisition: time, space, movement, and color. Table 6−1 summarizes the categories of symbols I found in each of these dimensions. In real life, these dimensions are closely interrelated; they cannot be neatly packaged and separated. Kepes (1969) writes, "The perception of physical reality cannot escape the quality of movement. The very understanding of spatial facts, the meaning of extensions, or distances, involves the notion of time—a fusion of space-time which is movement" (p. 179). And "to experience color," he adds, "is to interpret the very core of physical reality in terms of sensory qualities" (p. 134).

Because the space-time continuum is such an integral element of our existence, its influence on our literacy is inescapable. The relationship of our sense of personal time to the time sequences that are occurring around us are even considered by some philosophers to be the core of narrative plot (see Brockelman, 1985; Ricoeur, 1984; and Hillman, 1975). If we are indeed in the midst of a huge change in our

Table 6−1   Dimensions and Symbol Categories

Time	Space	Movement	Color
Time's arrow	Relationship of size	Multiple images	Record details
Time's cycle	Transparency	"As it happens"	Cultural
Words and pictures	Overlapping figures	Frozen moment	Light effects
	Mixed perspective	Metaphor	Metaphor
	Bird's-eye view	Action lines	Words and pictures
	Words and pictures	Pop-ups	
		Words and pictures	

present conception of time and space, as Jeremy Rifkin (1987) argues, what will the effects of "the new nanosecond culture" and the "bigger is better society" have on our literate behaviors? Each of the dimensions analyzed here opens up similar research avenues that invite further investigation.

Besides summarizing what categories occurred *within* each dimension, Table 6–1 also points out some similarities *across* dimensions. The appearance of a metaphor category, both in depicting color and movement, emphasizes the key role of metaphor in working out and expressing new meanings. "A metaphor, in short, tells us something new about reality" (Ricoeur, 1976, p. 53). When Graham created gaping jaws to express the impatient driving of a New York motorist or Sarah described a rotten pumpkin as orange mashed potatoes, they created metaphors in which the meanings of the pictures or words were extended beyond their familiar sense, thus telling us something new about reality. Graham and Sarah came to know something new, too—struggling to express through metaphor and analogy the meaning of something helps us come to know it (Berlin, 1978; and Ricoeur, 1977).

Most importantly, in every dimension I investigated, the children used words and pictures together to communicate their inner designs. When pop-ups or action lines didn't quite express all the aspects of movement the children had in mind, they often found that a strong verb could help. And when prepositions like *on* or *over* proved imprecise, other children found that a diagram, picture, or map could complement the words to make the message clearer. The way visual and verbal symbols worked together was not clear-cut. The children shifted back and forth, sometimes relying more on words and sometimes more on pictures. There appeared to be two main influences on which symbol system dominated a literacy event: the nature of the task and the cognitive bias of the child.

Over and over, I found that children shifted their strategies and their symbols depending on the task at hand. Consider, for example, the depiction of movement in the Rotten Jack journals. Although using pop-ups to express motion had been used by every child in the class, none used it to show the "falling down" motion of the pumpkin—it simply wasn't effective. When children *did* use this convention in their stories, it was a conscious choice: Paul didn't use pop-ups until he needed them to show his spaceship flying up across the page to visit aliens; Megan never used it in her witch story, but she found it effective to show her dog springing up or swinging on a trapeze.

The symbol systems that children used evolve to enable them to cope more efficiently with the task at hand. There were days when Kelly's writing booklet was filled with page after page of words and hastily scrawled illustrations when she wanted to tell about how she was learning to master the patterns in her math pattern-block book. On other mornings, her detailed drawings would convey almost all of the dimensions of a bus crashing into a tree, with the words clarifying certain elements after the pictures were complete.

A child's cognitive bias also influences the choice of symbol systems to some extent. Jerome Kagan (1987) believes that all of us are born with what he calls a "bias"; it might be a bias toward shyness or assertiveness, for example, or toward a more active or passive nature. These personality impulses are tempered and shaped by the culture and environment to which we are exposed. I believe we are also born with a *cognitive bias* in terms of visual and verbal thinking—not, as popular psychology would have it, in terms of right-brained/left-brained thinking, but along a continuum, where some of us tend to rely more on one than the other. Ming, for example, is much more likely to depend on pictures than on words across a range of tasks, while Ashley usually relies more on verbal solutions. Vera John-Steiner's (1985) work supports this view. In her analysis of creative processes, she found that children *do* have unique strategies and modes of thinking but that these modes of thought are altered early on by their environment. "One of the most important bases for the development of a preferred mode of thought," she declares, "is to be found in the prevalence of certain activities in childhood" (p. 35).

This study points the way, then, to a systematic investigation that would relate the workings of different symbol systems to different aspects of the task environment that confront an individual and would take into account the cognitive bias of that individual. Current symbolic systems theories fail to consider either of these aspects.

Besides the specific dimensions discussed in Chapters 2 through 5, other important themes recur. The most important of these implicit themes is the vital role of children's *intentionality* in their literacy. Children do not randomly make marks on paper; they have certain purposes as they work. They might be testing out or experimenting with how something will look on paper, for example, as Gwen did in her color mixing experiments; or they might be trying consciously to make something they know or have experienced clear to an audience, as Claudia did when she carefully drew all the windows of her bedroom so I would understand its spatial dimensions. What has been missing in many of the research studies on children's drawing and writing is a look at their intentions. Researchers need to listen to the children's accounts of the problems they have posed for themselves and recognize their processes for solving those problems. We need to look at their writing and drawing in the context in which it occurs and to take into account the children's intentions rather than continue to look at their solutions condescendingly from adultcentric viewpoints. Clearly, we can learn much more about Megan's abilities to depict motion when she *intends* to show a frog leaping through space than we would if we asked her—for no apparent reason—to draw a stick in its stages of flight after being thrown.

Linked to this intentionality finding is the prevalence—and the undeniable strength—of the children's *preplanning abilities*. Some children held a carefully sequenced set of plans in their mind, as Sally did in preparation for her story "The Ring." Although she didn't put words and pictures to paper until November, she told me she had been planning to write this story since she heard it, two months earlier! The following excerpt from my field notes (November 5, 1987) demonstrates many of the preplanning strategies I found in Sally's and other children's work:

Sally: I'm trying to figure out how to explain what a deli is.
Ruth: Is that because you're writing about a deli?
Sally: I was telling Debbie about what I was writing and it has a deli in it. It's an amazing story.
Ruth: Can you tell me about it?

Sally: OK, this is a true story. One time my mom was reading me the newspaper? And she said there was this part in it and this lady had a ring?

Ruth: Mmm-hmm?

Sally: And she lost her ring while she was working in the bakery? And she thought that she had lost it in a big crock of dough? So they searched the whole bakery, but they couldn't find it, and one time, while a different lady was, from the bakery, was eating with the lady from the deli, she... the lady from the bakery said, "Isn't it too bad about Anna's ring?" And then the lady in the deli said, "We found a ring in the back of our deli behind the refrigerator and we put it in a safe spot." So they quickly called up Anna, and they went down to the bakery, but the spot was too safe and they couldn't find it!

Ruth: Oh, no! You're kidding! And so you're gonna write about the story your mom read you from the newspaper?

Sally: Yup. My mom's gonna be reading me the newspaper... and I'm gonna write the whole story in this [stapled together pages of paper].

Ruth: And you're writing the title first?

Sally: Yup, "The Ring," 'cause I knew I was... keep it about the same thing.

Ruth: Uh-huh. So did your mom read you the newspaper story yesterday?

Sally: No, a pretty long time ago. [*I later found this front page human interest story in a September 1987 issue of* The Boston Globe.] But I was writing about Halloween because Halloween was coming up, and I thought after Halloween I would write about this.

Ruth: Can you tell me a little about what you're doing now?

Sally: Well, I'm drawing me and my mom's gonna be saying, my mom's gonna be reading me what's in the newspaper, and I'm gonna do pretend cursive, like this [*she scribbles on her writing folder cover*] with these wavy lines to look like the newspaper, 'cause it would take too long just to write little letters.... [*She draws and colors in her mom's feet.*] I was thinking before I was gonna write about the ring. I thought it would be fun to write about....

Ruth: So you're drawing the picture first?

Sally: Well, it helps me because when I'm drawing, it makes me think of so many ways I can say what's happening. I'm just thinking like, "Well, maybe I can say this... and that." I'm just thinking of what I'm gonna write while I'm drawing. But if I draw the words first, I don't know what I'm gonna write and I don't know what the picture's gonna look like.

This conversation with Sally shows the preplanning that occurred before she sat down to write and the planning that continued as she began to work. She knows the main idea of her story is about a ring, so that's the title she writes, even though she doesn't mention a ring until the third page of her story. She plans to draw her mother reading the newspaper and has considered what symbols she can use to effectively represent the small newsprint on the page. Sally is also aware of what strategies help her refine her thinking into words to put on the page; she knows the content, but needs to rehearse the words in her head, and she knows that drawing helps her do this.

These preplanning strategies—and many others—were prevalent throughout the classroom. Although some children, like Sally, drew part of their story first, others found it helpful to start by writing down words, then drawing the pictures they needed to accompany their story. Many needed to talk about their plans, rehearsing orally with neighbors before beginning to commit their messages to paper. Often, children had done some of their preplanning before coming to school, talking about possible topics with their families at home or on the bus on the way to school. Evidence like this argues against the contentions of researchers like Carl Bereiter (1980), who assert that primary school children do *not* preplan; this evidence calls instead for further investigations of the types of preplanning strategies children use and the conditions under which they occur.

One of the underlying themes that reoccurred throughout my research was the importance of the *influence of the electronic media* on the children's symbol weaving. The most obvious influences were in the form of certain cartoonlike conventions that the children picked up to some extent from books but more often from television or home videos: conventions like word bubbles, thought clouds, or action lines. Topics were influenced by what the children had been viewing: Ghostbusters adventures, Batman stories, "My Little Pony" episodes, and stories from the news, like earthquakes or oil tank explosions, were common in the children's writing folders. But more subtle influences were also important. The key role of movement in the children's writing and drawing may have some link to their constant exposure to the action- and motion-filled world of television, as their criticism of Sally's cartoon book hinted. The sense of time segments in Paul's T.V. story is another example of the impact of television programming practices on children's literacy. His sense of the way narration works with television images is also evident in this story: the narrator's voice is always on the bottom of the page, cuing the viewer to the picture and word content above. Paul's information about "good food" or "the bus crash" are carefully separated from the voice that reports, "After this message, we'll be right back," or "And now, back to Good Food." These less obvious influences also deserve further study.

Finally, the *role of the teacher*—the rhythm that she or he establishes in the structure and environment of the classroom, the values that are both explicit and implicit, the theories on which he or she bases day-to-day decisions (of a child's abilities and of how people learn), and his or her own literacy behaviors—have enormous influence on the emerging literacy of children. Every corner of Pat McLure's classroom gives clues to her learning theories and her broad definition of literacy. In March, for example, one large bulletin board was labeled "Art Gallery," with reproductions of Matisse's art, picture-book illustrators' drawings, a watercolor painting of a horse by one of last year's first-grade students, a collage made from wrapping paper and marker drawings by another six-year-old artist, and other diverse examples of artwork. Pat shows that she values the fine artists that abound in today's picture books as well as the classic masters—and she values the work of the artists who create daily in this workshop community.

Picture-book author-illustrator Trina Schart Hyman echoes e. e. cummings' claim that his paintings and poetry "love each other dearly" when she writes that her text and pictures "are absolutely married to each other" (Saul, 1988, p. 9). Pictures as well as words are important to human beings in their communication; we need to expand our narrow definition of literacy to include visual dimensions, and in so doing answer the call of researchers for the recognition of multi-literacies *and* ways these literacies can work to complement each other (see Gee, 1987; Greene, 1984; Klein, 1984; and Heath, 1983).

Most classrooms deny to children the very tools that adult authors find helpful in their work. Many writers, not just picture-book authors, rely on drawing to help them. The drafts and manuscripts for E. B. White's classic novel *Charlotte's Web* are full of sketches of pigs, barns, and of Charlotte herself, labeled with diagrams of the different parts of a spider, such as coxa and trochanter, which were later incorporated into the novel (Neumeyer, 1982). D. H. Lawrence found in oil painting a way to work out visual images that were later transformed into metaphor; John Dos Passos and William Faulkner's pencil sketches fill their notebooks, and writers as diverse as S. J. Perelman, Gabriel Garcia Marquez, and Flannery O'Connor began as cartoonists (Hjerter, 1986). In an account of his writing process, John Updike stresses how drawing and painting can be important tools for writers:

The subtleties of form and color, the distinctions of texture, the balances of volume, the principles of perspective and composition— all these are good for a future writer to experience and will help him to visualize his scenes, even to construct his personalities and to shape the invisible contentions and branchings of plot. A novel, like a cartoon, arranges stylized versions of people within a certain space; the graphic artist learns to organize and emphasize and this knowledge serves the writer. The volumes—cloven by line and patched by color—are imitated by those dramatic spaces the inner eye creates, as theatres for thoughts and fantasies. Unconscious, we dream within vivid spaces; when we read a book, we dream in a slightly different way, again slightly different from the way in which the writer dreamed. (Updike, 1986, p. 8)

It isn't just poets and novelists who rely on combinations of words and pictures to make their messages clear. Evans-Pritchard's ethnographies are full of his sketches "rimming, like visual footnotes, the edges of the text" (Geertz, 1988, p. 67). Stephen Jay Gould (1987) claims that pictures provided a key to his understanding of time's arrow and cycle and urges his readers not to consider the illustrations in his book as "pretty little trifles included only for aesthetic or commercial value" (p. 18). He argues that scholars have been too slow to recognize "another dimension to their traditional focus upon words alone" (p. 18). And other scientists, particularly M. J. Rudwick (1976), contend that primates are visual animals who rely on illustration. He focuses on the theme that illustration has a language and set of conventions all its own.

Curriculum directors will ask, if the language of literacy is expanded to include the visual dimension, how does this set of conventions and the sequence of development fit into the hierarchy of skills? Unfortunately, human development and literacy are messier than this. Tom Newkirk (1985) argues that there simply isn't a convenient scope and sequence into which educators can plug children; instead, we need to allow for considerable variability in the development of literacy.

Instead of looking for ways to isolate particular skills and plan mastery learning sequences, we can turn to classroom teachers who *are* successfully opening these new roads to literacy for their students. Besides early elementary teachers like Pat McLure, there are teachers at the upper-elementary, middle-school, and high-school levels who are expanding the dimensions of literacy in their classroom and learning with their students.

In writing about the process of teaching, Donald Murray (1982) stresses that a student must be given four freedoms: "the ability to find his own subject, to find his own evidence, to find his own audience, and to find his own form" (p. 142). Teacher-researchers like Cora Five (1986), Donna Lee and Paul Nelson (1988), and Linda Rief (1988) have all given these four freedoms to their students, including within the freedom of form the ability to use visual as well as verbal solutions to their problems.

In Cora Five's (1986) fifth-grade classroom, for example, the children often write her letters in response to the books they are reading, as well as journal entries to each other. But they are also encouraged, if they prefer, to sketch important parts of the books they are reading, map out characteristics, or create flow charts. "By collecting, sorting, reading, and re-reading their letters, maps, and sketches," Five writes, "I found for myself a much closer view of how children struggle and then succeed to find meaning in books. The process also kept me engaged in learning because it led me to new questions" (p. 405).

In the sixth-grade classroom they team teach, Donna Lee and Paul "Chip" Nelson (1988) also invite children to use whatever symbol system works best for them. They describe Andy as a "reluctant writer who had no idea that writing could turn to discovery. His belief that he had nothing to say entered into every conference and prevented him from ever writing unless forced to do so" (p. 7). Instead of focusing on the difficulties Andy had with written conventions, they instead validated the sketches that filled his writing folder, encouraging him to use these drawings to communicate the things he *did* know about—particularly fish. His careful pencil drawings illustrate his nonfiction piece "Salmon and Trout of the Squamscott," and his sketches are an integral part of his plans to cross-breed fish from a local river (Figure 6–1). His sixth-grade classmates' writing folders, too, are full of maps

Figure 6–1   Two of Andy's Fish Drawings

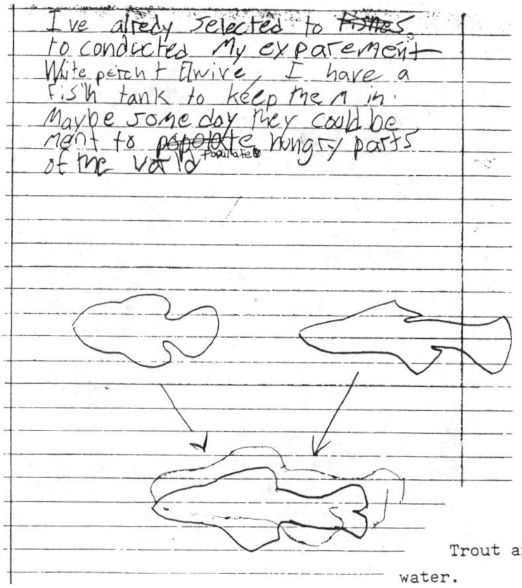

I've alredy selected to fishes
to conducted My experement
White perch + alwive, I have a
fish tank to keep men in.
Maybe some day they could be
nent to populate hungry parts
of the vorld

Chapter 2 - Trout

Trout are mainly fish that live in fresh
water.

There are three different types of trout
that live in the Squamscott River: the rainbow
trout, brook trout, and the brown trout.

A rainbow trout can be identified by the
bright colors on their side. The colors form
a rainbow.

Rainbow
Trout

Figure 6–2   Jim's "The Place Intact"

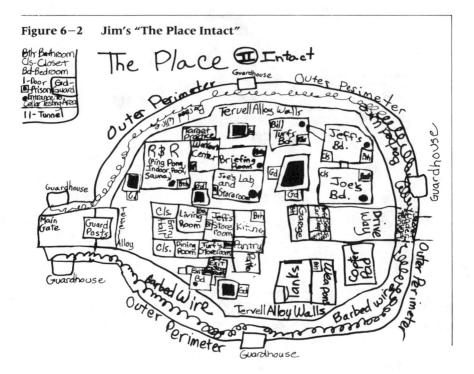

and diagrams, like the detailed layout drawn in Jim's "The Place Intact" (Figure 6–2) that accompanies his writing, or Grant's description of the way to fix a bicycle (Figure 6–3).

"With my help as a facilitator and as part of a writing community," writes Chip Nelson (1988), "the children are responsible for their own learning" (p. 8). One of the ways Chip acts as a facilitator is by surrounding the children with pictures and print. As in Pat McLure's classroom, the walls are covered with posters, charts, and graphs, and the children are immersed in the works of fine adult authors and illustrators. "Surround the children with literature," urges Donald Graves (1983), reporting the variety of connections children can make to their own work. The children in Donna and Chip's sixth-grade classroom are surrounded by the literature of master writers and illustrators, and aspects of their work turn up in the writing of the children, from Tad's Tolkein-like map of his fictitious world to the knights and damsels in Christine's novel who are dressed in intricate medieval costumes reminiscent of Trina Schart Hyman's artwork.

Figure 6–3   Grant's Instructions on Bicycle Repair

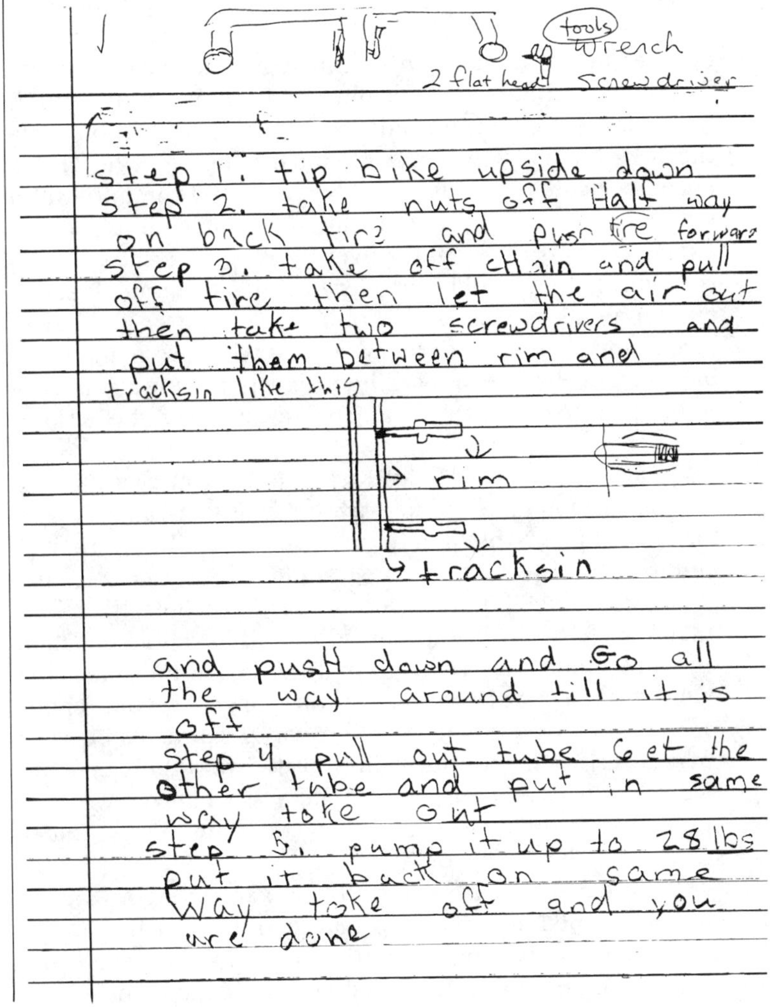

tools
wrench
2 flat head screwdriver

step 1. tip bike upside down
step 2. take nuts off Half way
on back tire and push tire forward
step 3. take off cHain and pull
off tire then let the air out
then take two screwdrivers and
put them between rim and
tracksin like this

→ rim

4 tracksin

and push down and Go all
the way around till it is
off
step 4. pull out tube Get the
other tube and put in same
way take out
step 5. pump it up to 28 lbs
put it back on same
Way take off and you
are done

The atmosphere in these classrooms encourages total communication in the students' literate behaviors. Much of the debate about children's preferred mode of thought has focused on diagnosing a learning style, then encouraging one particular mode. In the history of deaf education, a similar polarization occurred: some deaf educators believed solely in preparing their students for a hearing world, banning sign language and teaching lipreading and oral speech only; on the other end of the continuum were the educators who believed in teaching only American Sign Language. In the last decade, the school of total communication has gained prominence in deaf education; educators of this persuasion argue that their learning environments and teaching activities should encourage children to use whatever modes of communication will work best for them, including combinations of Sign Language, lipreading, and finger spelling. The idea of total communication should spill over in mainstream public school environments as well. This would allow children to learn to communicate in a range of modes and with a combination of media that will work best for them, experimenting and altering techniques to meet the changing demands of the tasks at hand.

Teacher-researcher Linda Rief (1988) encourages this total communication in her middle-school classrooms, and she finds that her students often rely on visual as well as verbal solutions. She reports that some students, for example, find photographs helpful tools for describing people they have interviewed. "In their journals, some kids have told me about studying photos they've taken in order to add the details that will create a vivid description on paper," Linda reports. "I've never given them directions or assignments that ask them to use pictures or drawings in the ways they have, but I've made it clear that they should use whatever works to communicate their messages, or to show me they've understood what they've read."

After reading *Romeo and Juliet*, for example, Alan's journal entry contained a comic-strip rendition of the parts he had read. "I had fun writing/illustrating in my log," he wrote, and the pages that followed reflected both his enjoyment and his understanding of the story (Figure 6−4).

Sandy, on the other hand, used words and pictures in quite another way: she chose to borrow the picture-book format of an old Dick and Jane reader to write about Ann Hutchinson's flight from Massachusetts because of religious persecution in her book entitled "Dick and Jane Visit the Massachusetts Bay Colony." Using the stylized words and pictures of this genre, she showed her knowledge of the

Figure 6–4   Alan's "Romeo and Juliet"

historical event she studied. Her readers learn about Ann Hutchinson's escape to Rhode Island through Dick and Jane's journey in the time machine they built "with a spatula, macaroni, paper mache . . . and the red wagon" (Figure 6–5).

Other examples, like Ann-Marie's autobiographical chart (Figure 6–6) or Stacy's porcupine brochure (Figure 6–7), which includes the "Eating Habits Poem" alongside the diagrammed "Characteristics," show the range of solutions and the strength of communication these teenagers demonstrate when literacy is viewed as a process of total communication.

These classrooms can give us the opportunity to see what is possible for students *and* for teachers. Drawing is not just for children who can't yet write fluently, and creating pictures is not just part of rehearsal for real writing. Images *at any age* are part of the serious business of making meaning—partners with words for communicating our inner designs.

Figure 6–5   Sandy's Dick and Jane Book

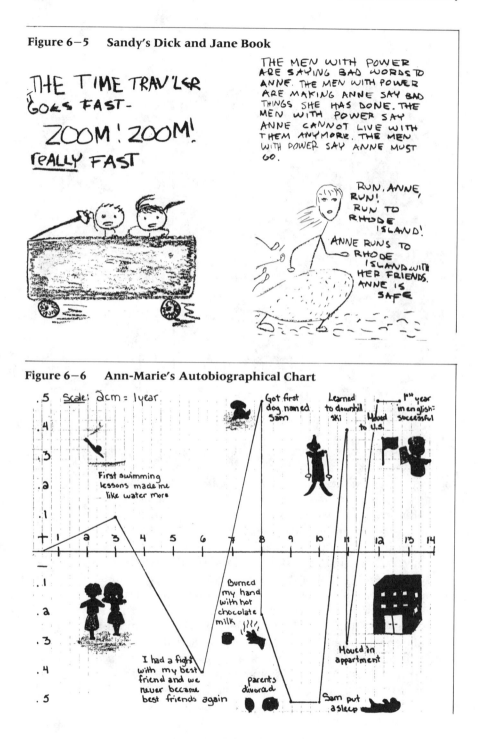

Figure 6–6   Ann-Marie's Autobiographical Chart

Figure 6–7   Stacy's Brochure (Excerpts)

EATING HABITS POEM

The eating habits of the porcupine,
Are really, quite honestly, truely devine.
In spring, she eats buds, twigs and leaves
And munches on acorns from the acorn trees.
Also, on the menu are wild onions and mushroom,
And also geraniums if there is enough room
She will wade in a pond, holding tail erect
And munch on a lilly pad without a fret
Salt is by far her most favorite treat,
And to get it she'll go through impossible feat.
How can she hold all this food? Do you ask?
Her 25 foot intestine preforms the hard task
Her large incissors gnaw as she sits on her haunches.
And bringing food up with her hand she sits quietly and maunches.
Her stomach can hold one pound of food.
which her large liver stores for the winter interlude.
When snow hits the ground and grasses are covered
She climbs up a tree and sits there: Hovered.
She gnaws on the bark in her thick coat she grew
And stays up there for days, stuck to it like glue.
Yes, this vegetarian is very unique.

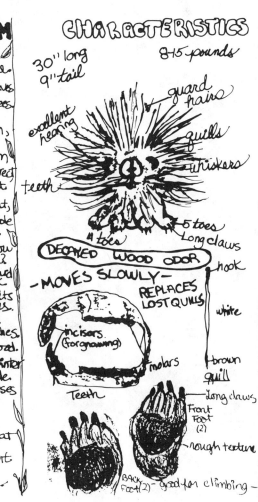

appendix

Classroom Context

Pat McLure's first-grade classroom emphasized the children's processes as well as their products. Her class embodied the literacy philosophies discussed in the work of writing process and whole language theorists such as Donald Graves, Lucy Calkins, Ken and Yetta Goodman, Jerry Harste, and Jane Hansen. This classroom, however, had its own variations, and, of course, a different classroom culture from year to year; therefore, the following descriptions and examples should prove helpful for readers who wish to understand the full context of the study.

On the first day of school, Pat explained the routine for the first part of the morning as she sat with the children in the meeting area (excerpt from field notes, September 2, 1987):

Pat: The first thing every day, we'll spend time writing.
Kelly: I like writing stories.
Pat: We made some booklets for you to choose from....
Kelly: We did this in kindergarten! We started big, then got smaller.
Ming: Mrs. Dunn [the kindergarten teacher] tricked us like that.
Pat: And I'll bring around folders for you to keep your writing in.
Ethan: And we can't bring them home.
TJ: Until the end of the year.
Kelly: Will we make books like those? [*She points to the carton of published books by child authors from last year.*]
Pat [*smiling*]: Yes.
[*Happy noises from the children.*]
Graham: I saw a book *that* small [*holds up fingers about one inch apart*].
Paul: I bet I could make one that small.

Megan: You'd only use one staple for that!

Pat: Books are different sizes...and they can be different colors, too. On most of the desks, there are crayons. There are some markers you can share, too. In the art area, there are more markers you can take to your desk to share. Try to use the pencils for the writing. It's easier to erase if you need to.

Ashley: I write a lot at home.

Nick: Me, too. I write and draw pictures at home.

Kelly: I have even more with pictures.

Ashley: I made a butterfly once, and cut it out and glued it on paper.

Pat: Well, that's what we'll do now—and tomorrow, first thing. Now, till the big hand is on the nine [15 minutes away] you can work on your writing, then we'll come back to the meeting area, and some of you may want to share.

During this morning writing time, Pat circulated around the room, conferring with children about the writing and drawing they were doing. Because she wished to establish a community in her class, she encouraged them from the start to turn to each other for help. Kelly is a child who likes to have a lot of attention, especially adult attention, but Pat made it clear to her that she needs to talk with the other children, not just the teacher, about her writing and drawing.

One morning early in September, Kelly saw that Pat was busy and turned to TJ, a returning veteran of last year's first grade, as she worked on her writing. First, she explained her drawing: "This is my brother with a stick running after me. I wanted people to know we were running, so I made them [the legs] up like that. My brother's funny. He likes to blend in with the woods. Sometimes we get lost when we play hide-and-seek."

TJ looked up from his writing, interested, and asked good, content-based questions. "How do you find him?" he began.

"Sometimes we find him by poking a stick in the woods. If it says, 'Ow,' it's Jacob."

TJ laughed. "When you do that, does he get mad?"

"No," Kelly shook her head. "'Cause he wants to be found."

"So did you ever not find him?"

Kelly thought a minute before answering. "Yeah, once it took till suppertime to find him."

"What place was he hiding in?" TJ probed, drawing out more information.

"Behind my climbing tree." Kelly turned back to her writing now, with lots to say in the next few pages, drawing the dark night and her family looking and calling for Jacob. She elaborated on her story with information brought out in her conference with TJ.

Just as children learn to depend on each other as well as the teacher, they also depend on the underlying structures of the class, which they soon internalize.

"The hand's on the two. Time for the meeting area." With these words, Susan put away her writing folder and headed for the meeting area where the class always met at 9:10 A.M. Without a word from Pat, the first graders were all closing folders, shuffling papers, and returning crayons to boxes. The routine had been established; by early fall, they knew what to expect. This was the time of day that the children shared their writing and received questions and comments from their classmates. Even at the beginning of the year, the children's simple stories, often pictures with one line of text, prompted participation from the class. Sometimes, the stories the children shared had no written text, but Pat and the other children accepted the drawing itself as the text.

Early in the year, for example, Jimmy shared his writing —a picture of his house, which he held up for the class to see, saying, "This is my house." Kelly commented that she liked his story, and several other children commented that they liked the picture. But other questions brought out more information about his house. Ming wanted to know why he decided to write about his house, for example, and when the discussion turned to how this house was different from his old house, many children joined in to comment about the merits of porches and the number of floors in houses, as this excerpt from my field notes (September 16, 1987) shows:

Jimmy: It's got a porch.

Pat: It's got a porch?

Megan: My house has a front porch, but it has stairs, but I never use them, because there's two sliding doors here and one here and I always slide right through down here. Because I have . . . and I don't want to go all the way around back here, and then down, I can just slip through there and go to my friend's house. She has a back door, too.

Brad: I have three floors.

Pat: Three floors?

Nick: I have four. I have a basement, a medium one, a upstairs, and then a attic.

Eugene: I've got a porch.

Nick: I have a porch, too.

Pat: Thank you for sharing your story, Jimmy. You did a nice job.

One of the most important aspects of these sessions was the event itself. It gave children a chance to validate their stories and an opportunity to talk and to further refine their thinking. In these whole-class sharing sessions, the written and drawn text was often a kind of conversation starter, and the opportunity to speak was the most important thing. (For an analysis of the whole-class sharing sessions in Pat McLure's first-grade classroom and their importance in her language arts curriculum, see Hubbard, 1985b.)

After the children shared their pieces, the class began its "first working time." This was primarily a reading time, especially on Monday mornings, when the children chose a new book to practice reading and recorded that choice in their reading folders. (For an example of a book list, see Figure A−1.) Pat introduced the book list in early October, adding an explanation of them to her usual directions:

Figure A−1   A Book List

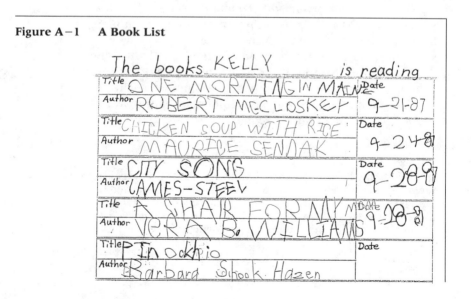

Pat: We need to have people who are ready for listening to directions. It's Monday morning and people need to find a new book to work on for their reading work. They need to write the title and the author on the book list, and today's date because you are choosing it. In your folder, this is your book list [*shows it*]. That's where you need to write your title and the author and the date that you choose it. Today is the day you choose it. Do not do any other writing about the book. You aren't doing the sentence paper, just choosing a book and practicing reading it. You need to use today's working time to practice reading.

During the rest of the week, the children practiced reading their books with a friend. They then wrote a "sentence paper" about the book. On these sentence papers, the children were expected to "tell something about the book," and they usually used a combination of words and pictures to do this (Figure A—2).

Finally, they shared their books in small group reading conferences with a few other children and Pat. In these conferences, each child brought the book he or she was reading

---

Figure A—2   Telling About the Book. A: Ming—"In the house, it looks like a woods." B: Graham—"This book is good for children who are starting to read books because the writing is not too big or too small."

a

b

and read a section of it, or the whole thing if it was short. The others asked questions and made comments about the book, sometimes focusing their discussions on the content, other times discussing the strategies they used in order to be able to read it. One morning, I joined Nick, Paul, and Gwen as they shared their reading with Pat. Nick had chosen the group members, so he was the designated leader (excerpt from field notes, September 24, 1987):

[*Some children come over to ask Pat a question.*]

Pat: I'm trying to have a reading group. You don't bother me unless it's an emergency. Nick, who's first?

Nick: Paul, then me, then Gwen.

Paul: A Ghost Story. I already read it to the whole class. I'll tell you the title first. [*He reads it, then shows pictures, with lots of exclamations, "See? See?"*]

Gwen: I see it.

Pat: I see it.

Paul [*reads the whole ghost story, then, in a louder voice, ends with*]: "He's got ya!"

Pat: I like the way you made your voice sound scary, then surprised at the end.

Nick: How did you learn to read it?

Paul: I picked it up during quiet reading time. I couldn't read it all, then I tried again and I got a few more words, and then the third time, I read it all.

Gwen: Why did you pick it?

Paul: I just explained. I picked it on the red rug. It was just quiet reading.

Pat: I think you read another one of the same set. *When It Rains, It Pours*. Do you like that kind of book?

Paul: It was in a different box. I read two other scary ones. I think they're all by the same man.

Pat: Thank you. Nick?

[*Nick shares the pictures in* Creatures Small and Furry.]

The sharing group continued, with each child having a turn to share and receive the questions and comments of the others in the group.

Sometimes, the children only read during this "working time," but more often they had two tasks to complete. One day, for example, Pat said, "For our working time today, you need to think about reading work and math work. Some people have some booklets in their math folders. For your reading work, some more people will have turns to share at the round table, and you need to start working on your sentence papers. So, your sentence papers, your math papers, and some people will be sharing at the round table. You can either start with math or reading" (Field notes, October 22, 1987).

This working time continued until 10:00, when the children knew it was time to put away what they had been working on and have their morning snack before going out to play for recess at 10:15.

Their morning schedule continued with a whole-class reading and sharing session after recess. One child signed up every day for this session and he or she read either a part of a book or the entire story, if it was short. Just as in the writing share sessions, the reader of the story then accepted comments and questions from the others in the class. One morning in October, Megan read a picture book to the class about being lost (field notes, October 27, 1987):

Megan [*reads*]: "Lost. Lost. I don't want an ice cream. I want my daddy. I don't want a rabbit. I want my daddy. I don't want a ride. I want my daddy. I want my dad. There he is! Daddy, daddy. Don't get lost again, daddy." It was funny when I showed you that, 'cause she got lost! I bet it was funny when I showed you this.

Paul: That's just white paper with letters and stuff.

Megan: I know. Comments and questions? Joshua?

Joshua: Why did you pick that book?

Megan: Well, it's the first one I saw. Ethan?

Ethan: I like the part where he says, "I don't want a rabbit. I want my daddy."

Megan: Claudia?

Claudia: I like how you showed . . .

Megan: What?

Jenny [*finishing for Claudia*]: I like how you showed the pictures.

Claudia: No!

Sarah: The story?

Claudia: Right.

Megan: Sarah?

Sarah: I like how you showed the pictures. They're—you need them.

Megan: Yeah, like, I think this one's really a picture thing and when it's in front up here you don't need that word in there. You

don't need the word, you don't need it for a lot of things, like,
let me see. The first page, it looks like he's lost without saying lost.
Sally?

Sally: I like the part where he says, "Don't get lost again, daddy!" . . .

Ruth: Have you ever been lost, Megan?

Megan: Once I thought I was lost, but my dad always finds me.

Ruth: How did he find you?

Megan: He was turning around corners really fast and I wanted to
follow, but I got lost.

Paul: I got lost a million times in all these stores.

In this fairly typical share session, the children asked
Megan how she chose the book, commented on their favorite
parts, discussed the choices of both words and pictures, and
related their own personal experiences to the events in the
story. Some of the same picture books and stories became
class favorites and were repeated often, building the confidence
in some readers to pick up those books on their own and
choose them to add to their book lists.

After this whole-class reading share, the class usually had
another "working time" similar to the one just before snack
and recess. Again, the children typically had a choice of the
order in which to complete their tasks, which were usually
math and reading but might also be special projects, such as
the Rotten Jack unit (explained in detail in Chapter 3).

As the activities described in this section show, the classroom
community consisted of both the teacher and the children.
Although Pat McLure was the recognized authority in this
social hierarchy, she shared most of the activities with the
children, and much of the decision making was negotiated;
within the classroom structure, the children had a great deal
of responsibility for their learning.

references

Abbott, E. A. [1884] 1963. *Flatland: A romance of many dimensions.* 5th ed. New York: Harper & Row.

Abel, E. 1980. Redefining the sister arts: Baudelaire's response to the art of Delacroix. In W. J. T. Mitchell (Ed.), *The language of images* (pp. 37–58). Chicago: The University of Chicago Press.

Agar, M. 1980. *The professional stranger.* New York: Academic Press.

Akhundov, M. D. 1986. *Conceptions of space and time.* Cambridge: The MIT Press.

Arendt, H. 1976. *The life of the mind: Thinking* (Vol. I). New York: Harcourt Brace Jovanovich.

Aries, P. 1962. *Centuries of childhood.* New York: Alfred A. Knopf.

Arnheim, R. 1969. *Visual thinking.* Berkeley, CA: University of California Press.

Arnheim, R. 1974. *Art and visual perception: A psychology of the creative eye.* Berkeley: University of California Press.

Augustine. 1966. *The confessions of St. Augustine.* (E. B. Pusey, Trans.) New York: Dutton.

Axtell, J. 1976. *The school upon the hill.* New York: Norton.

Bateson, G. 1972. *Steps to an ecology of mind.* New York: Ballantine.

Beekman, T. 1986. Stepping inside: On participant experience and bodily presence in the field. *Journal of Education, 3,* 39–45.

Bereiter, C. 1980. Development in writing. In L. Gregg & E. Steinberg (Eds.), *Cognitive processes in writing.* Hillsdale, NJ: Lawrence Erlbaum.

Berger, P. L., & Luckmann, T. 1966. *The social construction of reality: A treatise in the sociology of knowledge.* Garden City, NY: Doubleday.

Berlin, I. 1978. Sir Isaiah Berlin on men of ideas and children's puzzles. *The Listener.* January 26.

Bernstein, R. J. 1983. *Beyond objectivity and relativity: Science, hermeneutics, and praxis.* Philadelphia: University of Pennsylvannia Press.

Black, J. 1981. Are young children really egocentric? *Young Children, 36,* 51–55.

Bloch, R. H. 1978. American feminine ideas in transition: The rise of the moral mother, 1785–1815. *Feminist Studies, 4,* 101–126.

Boas, F. 1955. *Primitive Art.* New York: Dover Publications.

Booth, W. 1974. *Modern dogma and the rhetoric of assent.* Chicago: University of Chicago Press.

Bower, T. G. 1966. The visual world of infants. *Scientific American, 215,* 90.

Brockelman, P. 1985. *Time and self: Phenomenological explorations.* New York: The Crossroads Publishing Company and Scholars Press.

Bruner, J. 1966. *Toward a theory of instruction.* Cambridge: Harvard University Press.

Bruner, J. 1983. *Child's talk: Learning to use language.* New York: W. W. Norton.

Burns, R., & Kaufman, S. H. 1972. *Actions, styles, and symbols in kinetic family drawings (K-F-D): An interpretive manual.* New York: Brunner/Mazel.

Child, I., Hansen, J., & Hornbeck, F. 1968. Age and sex differences in children's color preferences. *Child Development, 39,* 237–247.

Clark, H. H., Carpenter. P. A., & Just, M. A. 1973. On the meeting of semantics and perception. In W. G. Chase (Ed.), *Visual information processing* (pp. 311–382). New York: Academic Press.

Coles, R. 1986. *The moral lives of children.* Boston: Atlantic Monthly Press.

Cook-Gumperz, J. 1986. Caught in a web of words: Some considerations on language socialization and language acquisition. In J. Cook-Gumperz, W. Corsaro, and J. Streeck (Eds.), *Children's worlds and children's language* (pp. 37–64). New York: Moyten de Grutyer.

Cooper, L. A. & Shepherd, R. N. 1973. Chronometric studies of the rotation of mental images. In W. G. Chase (Ed.), *Visual information processing* (pp. 75–176). New York: Academic Press.

Corcoran, A. 1954. Color usage in nursery school painting. *Child Development, 25,* 107–113.

Corsaro, W. 1981. Entering the child's world: Research strategies for field entry and data collection in a pre-school setting. In J. Green and C. Wallett (Eds.), *Ethnography and language in educational settings* (pp. 117–146). Norwood, NJ: Ablex Press.

Dean, A. L. 1976. The structure of imagery. *Child Development, 47,* 949–958.

Doheny-Farina, S. 1986. Writing in an emerging organization: An ethnographic study. *Written Communication, 3,* 158–185.

Donaldson, M. 1978. *Children's minds.* New York: W. W. Norton.

Duncan, H. F., Gourlay, N., & Hudson, W. 1973. *A study of pictorial perception among Bantu and White primary school children in South Africa.* Johannesburg: Witwatersrand University Press.

Eisenstein. E. 1979. *The printing press as an agent of change.* New York: Cambridge University Press.

Eisner, E. 1976. *The arts, human development, and education.* Berkeley. CA: McCutchan Publishing Corporation.

Five, C. L. 1986. Fifth graders respond to a changed reading program. *Harvard Educational Review, 56,* 395–405.

Flaherty, M. 1987. Multiple realities and the experience of duration. *The Sociological Quarterly, 28,* 313–326.

Foulke, A. 1956. *Un sens a la vie* [A sense of life]. (A. Foulke, Trans.) Paris: Gallimard Editions.

Fraser, J. T. 1966. *The voices of time.* New York: George Braziller.

Fraser. J. T. 1975. *Of time, passion, and knowledge.* New York: George Braziller.

Freeman, N. 1977. How children try to plan drawings. In G. Butterworth (Ed.), *The child's representation of the world* (pp. 3–30). New York: Plenum.

Freeman, N. 1980. *Strategies of representation in young children.* London: Academic Press.

Freidrich, O. 1983. What do babies know? *Time.* August 15. pp. 52–59.

Friedman, S., & Stevenson, M. 1980. Perception of motion in pictures. In M. Hagen (Ed.), *The perception of pictures.* (Vol. I, pp. 225–254.) New York: Academic Press.

Gardner, H. 1980. *Artful scribbles: The significance of children's drawings.* New York: Basic Books.

Gardner, H. 1982. *Art, mind, and brain: A cognitive approach to creativity.* New York: Basic Books.

Gee. J. P. 1987. *What is literacy?* Paper presented at the Planning Session for the Literacies Institute, Cambridge, MA. October.

Geertz, C. 1983. *Local knowledge: Further essays in interpretive anthropology.* New York: Basic Books.

Geertz, C. 1988. *Works and lives: The anthropologist as author.* Stanford, CA: Stanford University Press.

Gelman, R. 1981. Preschool thought. In M. Hetherington & R. D. Parke (Eds.), *Contemporary readings in child psychology* (pp. 159–165). New York: McGraw-Hill.

Gibson, E. 1969. *Principles of perceptual learning and development.* New York: Appleton-Century-Crofts.

Gibson, J. J. 1966. *The senses considered as perceptual systems.* Boston: Houghton Mifflin.

Gibson, J., & Yonas, P. 1968. A new theory of scribbling and drawing in children. In H, Levin, E. J. Gibson, & J. J. Gibson (Eds.), *The analysis of reading skill.* Washington, DC: U.S. Department of Health, Education, and Welfare, Office of Education. (Final Report)

Glaser, B., & Strauss, A. 1967. *The discovery of grounded theory: Strategies for grounded research.* New York: Aldine Publishing.

Goldstone, B. 1986. Views of childhood in children's literature over time. *Language Arts, 63,* 791–797.

Gombrich, E. 1961. *Art and illusion: A study in the psychology of pictorial representation.* New York: Pantheon Books.

Gombrich, E. 1980. Standards of truth: The arrested image and the moving eye. In W. Mitchell (Ed.), *The language of images* (pp. 181–218). Chicago: The University of Chicago Press.

Goodman, N. 1968. *Languages of art: An approach to a theory of symbols.* Indianapolis: Bobbs-Merrill.

Goodnow, J. J. 1978. Visible thinking: Cognitive aspects of change in drawings. *Child Development, 49,* 637–641.

Gould, S. J. 1987. *Time's arrow, time's cycle.* Cambridge: Harvard University Press.

Graves, D. H. 1983. *Writing: Teachers and children at work.* Portsmouth, NH: Heinemann.

Greene, M. 1984. The art of being present: Educating for aesthetic encounters. *Journal of Education, 166,* 123–135.

Gregory, R. 1970. *The intelligent eye.* New York: McGraw-Hill.

Grumet, M. R. 1986. The lie of the child redeemer. *Journal of Education 168,* 87–97.

Haber, R. 1966. Nature of the effect of set on perception. *Psychological Review, 73,* 335–351.

Hall, E. T. 1959. *The silent language.* Westport, CT: Greenwood Press.

Hall, E. T. 1983. *The dance of life.* New York: Anchor/Doubleday.

Hansen, J. 1987. *When writers read.* Portsmouth, NH: Heinemann.

Hansen, J., & Graves, D. H. 1986. Do you know what backstrung means? *The Reading Teacher, 39,* 807–812.

Harste, J., & Rowe, D. 1986. Metalinguistic awareness in writing and reading: The young child as curricular informant. In D. Yaden and S. Templeton (Eds.), *Metalinguistic awareness and beginning literacy: Conceptualizing what it means to read and write* (pp. 235–256). Portsmouth, NH: Heinemann.

Harste, J., Woodward, V., & Burke, C. 1984. *Language stories and literacy lessons.* Portsmouth, NH: Heinemann.

Hayakawa, S. I. 1969. The revision of vision. In G. Kepes (Ed.), *The Language of vision* (pp. 8–10). Chicago: Paul Theobald.

Heath, S. B. 1983. *Ways with words: Language, life, and work in communities and classrooms.* New York: Cambridge University Press.

Heshesius, L. 1986. Pedagogy, special education, and the lives of young children: A critical and futuristic perspective. *Journal of Education, 168,* 25–37.

Hillman, J. 1975. The fiction of case history: A round. In J. B. Wiggins (Ed.), *Religion as story* (pp. 129–138). New York: Harper & Row.

Hjerter, K. G. 1986. *Doubly gifted: The author as visual artist.* New York: Harry N. Abrams.

Holland, N. 1968. *The dynamics of literary response.* New York: Oxford University Press.

Hubbard, R. 1985a. A day in the life of. . . In R. Hubbard & D. Stratton (Eds.), *Teachers and learners.* Durham, NH: Writing Process Lab at University of New Hampshire.

Hubbard, R. 1985b. Write-and-tell. *Language Arts, 62,* 624–630.

Hubbard, R. 1987. Transferring images: Not just glued on the page. *Young Children, 42,* 60–67.

Hudson, W. 1960. Pictorial depth perception in subcultural groups in Africa. *Journal of Social Psychology, 52,* 183–208.

Hughes, M., & Grieve, R. 1979. Interpretation of bizarre questions in five- and seven-year-old children. *Cognition, 8*, 73–82.

Isaacs, S. 1930. *Intellectual growth in young children.* New York: Harcourt and Brace.

Jenks, C. 1982. *The sociology of children.* London: Batsford.
John-Steiner, V. 1985. *Notebooks of the mind.* Albuquerque, NM: University of New Mexico Press.

Kagan, J. 1984. *The nature of the child.* New York: Basic Books.
Kagan, J. (Speaker) 1987. University of New Hampshire Psychology Department Colloquia Series (Videotape Recording). Durham, NH: University of New Hampshire Psychology Department.
Kaufmann, G. 1985. A theory of symbolic representation in problem solving. *Journal of Mental Imagery, 9*, 51–70.
Kennedy, J. M., & Ross, A. S. 1975. Outline picture perception by the Songe of Papua. *Perception, 4*, 391–406.
Kepes, G. 1969. *Language of vision.* Chicago: Paul Theobald.
Kessen, N. 1979. The American child and other cultural inventions. *American Psychologist, 34*, 815–820.
Klein, M. 1984. Four minutes till midnight. *Journal of education, 166*, 170–187.
Kosslyn, S. 1980. *Image and mind.* Cambridge: Harvard University Press.
Kosslyn, S. 1981. The medium and message in mental imagery. *Psychological Review, 1*, 46–66.
Kreitler, H., & Kreitler, S. 1972. *Psychology of the arts.* Durham, NC: Duke University Press.

Langer, S. 1942. *Philosophy in a new key.* Cambridge: Harvard University Press.
Lawler, C. O., & Lawler, E. E. 1965. Color-mood associations in young children. *The Journal of Genetic Psychology, 107*, 29–32.
Lee, D. 1988. *Emotions unleashed.* Paper presented at the annual conference of the National Council of Teachers of English, Boston, MA. March.
LeFevre, K. B. 1987. *Invention as a social act.* Carbondale, Illinois: Southern Illinois University Press.
Light, P. 1979. *The development of social sensitivity.* New York: Cambridge University Press.
Lionni, L. 1984. Before images. *The Horn Book*, pp. 726–734.
Locke, J. 1968. *Some thoughts concerning education.* From. J. L. Axtell's modern edition. New York: Cambridge University Press.

McGarrigle, J., & Donaldson, M. 1974. Conservation accidents. *Cognition, 3*, 341–350.
McLure, P. 1987. *What they know: A look at children's early writing.* Paper presented at the meeting of the National Association for the Education of Young Children, Portland, ME. May.

Malinowski, B. 1922. *Argonauts of the Western Pacific*. London: Routledge.

Maurer, D. M., & Maurer, C. E. 1976. Newborn babies see better than you think. *Psychology Today, 10*, 85−88.

Mead, M., & Wolfenstein, M. (Eds.). 1955. *Childhood in contemporary cultures*. Chicago: University of Chicago Press.

Meyrowitz, J. 1985. *No sense of place: The impact of electronic media on social behavior*. New York: Oxford University Press.

Miles, M. B., & Huberman, A. M. 1984. *Qualitative data analysis: A sourcebook of new methods*. Beverly Hills, CA: Sage Publications.

Miller, B. 1987. *Types of worlds*. Unpublished dissertation pilot study, University of New Hampshire, Durham, NH.

Murray, D. M. 1982. *Learning by teaching*. Portsmouth, NH: Boynton/ Cook.

Nelson, P. 1988. *Who's in control here?* Paper presented at the annual conference for the National Council of Teachers of English, Boston, MA. March.

Neumeyer, P. F. 1982. The creation of *Charlotte's Web*: From drafts to book. *The Horn Book*, 489−493.

Newkirk, T. 1985. The hedgehog or the fox. *Language Arts, 62*, 593−603.

Olson, R. 1975. Children's sensitivity to pictorial depth information. *Perception and Psychophysics, 17*, 59−64.

Paivio, A. 1971. *Imagery and verbal processes*. New York: Holt.

Paivio, A. 1983. The mind's eye in art and science. *Poetics, 12*, 1−18.

Piaget, J. 1945. Time perception in children. In J. T. Fraser (Ed.) (B. Montgomery, Trans.), *The voices of time* (pp. 202−216). New York: George Braziller.

Piaget, J., & Inhelder, B. 1967. *The child's concept of space*. New York: Norton Library.

Piaget, J., & Inhelder, B. 1971. *Mental imagery of the child*. New York: Basic Books.

Postman, N. 1981. Disappearing childhood. *Childhood Education, 58*, 66−68.

Ricoeur, P. 1976. *Interpretation theory: Discourse and the surplus of meaning*. Fort Worth, TX: Texas Christian University.

Ricoeur, P. 1977. *The rule of metaphor* (R. Czerny, trans.). Toronto: University of Toronto Press.

Ricoeur, P. 1984. *Time and narrative* (K. McLaughlin & D. Pellauer, trans.). Chicago: University of Chicago Press.

Rief, L. 1988. Personal communication. March.

Rifkin, J. 1987. *Time wars: The primary conflict in human history*. New York: Henry Holt.

Rorschach, H. 1951. *Psychodiagnostics*. (5th ed.). Bern & Stuttgart: Hans Huber.

Rosenblatt, L. 1978. *The reader, the text, and the poem: The transactional theory of the literary work.* Carbondale, IL: Southern Illinois University Press.

Rudwick, M. J. 1975. Caricature as a source for the history of science: De La Beche's anti-Lyellian sketches of 1831. *Isis, 66,* 534–560.

Rudwick, M. J. 1976. The emergence of a visual language for geological science, 1760–1840. *History of Science, 14,* 149–195.

Saint-Exupéry, A. 1943. *The little prince.* New York: Harcourt Brace Jovanovich.

Sapir, E. 1921. *Language.* New York: Harcourt Brace.

Saul, W. 1988. Once-upon-a-time artist in the land of now: An interview with Trina Schart Hyman. *The New Advocate, 1,* 8–17.

Schatzman, L., & Strauss, A. 1973. *Field research: strategies for natural sociology.* Englewood Cliffs, NJ: Prentice-Hall.

Shatz, M. 1977. The relationship between cognitive processes and the development of social communication skills. In C. Keasey (Ed.), *Social Cognitive Development.* Lincoln, NE: University of Nebraska Press.

Slater, P. G. 1977. *Children in the New England mind.* Hamden, CT: Archon Books.

Speier, M. 1976. The adult ideological viewpoint in studies of childhood. In A. Skolmuk (Ed.), *Rethinking children.* Boston: Little, Brown.

Spitz, R. A. 1965. *The first year of life.* New York: International Universities Press.

Spradley, J. 1979. *The ethnographic interview.* New York: Holt, Rinehart, and Winston.

Stea, D., & Blaut, J. M. 1973. Some preliminary observations on spatial learning in school children. In R. M. Downs & D. Stea (Eds.), *Image and environment* (pp. 226–234). Chicago: Aldine.

Stern, D. 1985. *The interpersonal world of the child: A view from psychoanalysis and developmental psychology.* New York: Basic Books.

Stone, L. 1977. The family, sex, and marriage in England 1500–1800. New York: Harper & Row.

Summerfield. G. 1984. *Fantasy and reason: Children's literature in the eighteenth century.* London: Methuen.

Thass-Theinemann, T. 1968. *Symbolic behavior.* New York: Washington Square Press.

Tizard, B., & Hughes, M. 1984. *Young children learning.* Cambridge: Harvard University Press.

Tuan, Y. 1977. *Space and place: The perspective of experience.* Minneapolis: University of Minnesota Press.

Updike, J. 1986. Foreword. In K. Hjerter (Ed.), *Doubly gifted: The author as visual artist* (pp. 7–9), New York: Henry N. Abrams.

Valentine, D. 1962. *The experimental psychology of beauty*. London: The Camelot Press.

Vygotsky, L. 1962. *Thought and language*. Cambridge: The MIT Press.

Vygotsky, L. 1978. *Mind in society: The development of higher psychological processes*. Cambridge: Harvard University Press.

Wadsworth, B. J. 1984. *Piaget's theories of cognitive and affective development*. New York: Longman.

Ward, J. L. 1979. A piece of the action: Moving figures in still pictures. In C. Nodine & D. Fisher (Eds.), *Perception and pictorial representation* (pp. 246–271). New York: Praeger.

White, S., & White, B. 1980. *Pathways of discovery*. London: Harper & Row.

Whorf, B. 1936. An American Indian model of the universe. In R. M. Gale (Ed.), *The philosophy of time: A collection of essays* (pp. 378–386). London: Macmillan.

Whorf, B. 1953. Linguistic factors in the terminology of Hopi architecture. *International Journal of American Linguistics, 19*, 701–745.

Whorf, B. 1956. *Language, thought, and reality*. Cambridge: The MIT Press.

Winner, E. 1982. *Invented worlds: The psychology of the arts*. Cambridge: Harvard University Press.

Winter, W. 1963. The perception of safety posters by Bantu industrial workers. *Psychologica Africana, 10*, 127–135.

Wishy, B. 1968. *The child and the republic*. Philadelphia: University of Pennsylvania Press.

Yonas, A., & Hagen, M. 1973. Effects of static and motion parallax depth information on perception of size in children and adults. *Journal of Experimental Child Psychology, 15*, 254–265.

Yonas, A., & Pick, H. J. 1975. An approach to the study of infant space perception. In L. Cohen & P. Salapatek (Eds.), *Infant perception: From sensation to cognition* (pp. 3–28). New York: Academic Press.